Creative Activities for the Secondary Classroom

Other titles in the series

Drinkwater: *Games and Activities for Primary Modern Foreign Languages*

Barron: *Practical Ideas, Games and Activities for the Primary Classroom*

Allen: *Games, Ideas and Activities for Primary PE*

Dabell: *Games, Ideas and Activities for Primary Mathematics*

Coulson and Cousins: *Games, Ideas and Activities for Early Years Phonics*

Minto: *Games, Ideas and Activities for Primary Music*

Green: *Games, Ideas and Activities for Primary Humanities*

Barron: *Games, Ideas and Activities for Learning Outside the Primary Classroom*

Theodorou: *Games, Ideas and Activities for Primary Drama*

Creative Activities
for the **Secondary**
Classroom

Mark Labrow

Longman
is an imprint of

Harlow, England • London • New York • Boston • San Francisco • Toronto
Sydney • Tokyo • Singapore • Hong Kong • Seoul • Taipei • New Delhi
Cape Town • Madrid • Mexico City • Amsterdam • Munich • Paris • Milan

PEARSON EDUCATION LIMITED
Edinburgh Gate
Harlow CM20 2JE
United Kingdom
Tel: +44 (0)1279 623623
Fax: +44 (0)1279 431059
Website: www.pearsoned.co.uk

First edition published in Great Britain in 2009

© Pearson Education Limited 2009

The right of Mark Labrow to be identified as author of this work has
been asserted by him in accordance with the Copyright, Designs and Patents Act 1988.

ISBN: 978-1-4082-2557-8

British Library Cataloguing in Publication Data
A CIP catalogue record for this book can be obtained from the British Library

Library of Congress Cataloging in Publication Data
Labrow, Mark.
  Creative activities for the secondary classroom / Mark Labrow.
     p.cm. – (Classroom gems)
  ISBN 978-1-4082-2557-8 (pbk.)
1. Creative thinking – Activity programs. 2. Drama. 2. Drama– Study and teaching (Secondary) –
Activity programs. 3. Education, Secondary – Activity programs. 1. Title.
  LB1062.L32 2010
  373.1102–dc22

                        2009034144

10 9 8 7 6 5 4 3 2 1
13 12 11 10 09

Set by 30 in 8.5/12pt Newsgothic BT
Printed and bound in Great Britain by Henry Ling Ltd., at the Dorset Press, Dorchester, Dorset

The Publisher's policy is to use paper manufactured from sustainable forests.

Contents

Foreword   vii
Introduction   ix

Chapter 1 Developing a
Sense of Team   1

    Introduction   2
    Name Me Thrice   3
    Name Tag   4
    Amazing Adjective Action
    Names   5
    Know Your Place   6
    Cat and Mouse   7
    Air Ball   8
    Bucket Ball   9
    5 4 3 2 1   11
    Triangle Tag   13
    Shuffle Monster   14
    Fill My Chair   16
    Cross-fire   17
    Negotiate   18
    Rules of Engagement   20
    Machines   21
    Own Goal   23
    Agree–Disagree Continuum   25
    The Flock   26
    Balancing the Stage   27
    Verbal Artist   29
    Mirrors   30
    Mirrors – Guess Who?   32
    Mirrors – Whisper on the Wind 34
    Mirrors – House of Fun   36
    Appliances   38

Advertise Me   40
Contract and Expand   42
Invisible Tug of War   44
Spell TEAM   46
The Game   48
Trust Walk   49
Trust Circle   51
Trust Fall   52
Trust Lift   54
Object Minefield   55
The Hand of Hypnosis   57

Chapter 2 Developing
Focus and Concentration   61

    Introduction   62
    1, 2, 3   63
    1 to 20   65
    Stop – Go   66
    Big Booty   68
    Yes Torpedo   70
    Rag Tail   71
    Catch it – Drop it   72
    Person to Person   73
    Fuzzy Duck   74
    Zip, Zap, Boing   75
    One Step Back   77
    Prisoner   79
    Bang!   81
    Sticks   82
    Brain Flop   84
    Focus Line Up   85
    Ha!   87
    The Impulse to Go   89

Chapter 3 Developing
Spontaneity 93

Introduction 94
What's in the Box? 95
Alliteration 96
Word Association 98
Rhyme Time 100
Shift 102
What are you Doing? 103
What the Audience Want 104
Sound Ball 106
Arms Through 108
Last Letter 110
I am a Sandwich 112
Word Up 114
Slide Show 115
Translator 117
Foreign Film 118
Dubbing 119
Fictionary 120
Die 121

Chapter 4 Developing
Scenes and Stories 125

Introduction 126
One Word Story/
Conversations 127
Alphabet 129
Hot Seating 131
Role on the Wall 133
Still Images 134
The Ripple 135
Sculpting 136
Thought Tracking 139
Conscience Alley 140
Diary Entry 142
Words of Wisdom 143
Cross Fade 145
Character Bridge 146

N.S.E.W. 147
Group Monologue 149
Photo Fit 151
Soundscape 153
Dreamscape 155
Ten-word Cascade 157
Hidden Thoughts 159
Park Bench 161
A Scene with no 'S' 163
What's a Question? 165
Every Other Question 166
Last Letter Scenes 168
The Creative Touch 170
Freeze Tag 171
Typewriter 172
Sixty-second Trailer 173
Rooms 175
Emotional Grid 177
Sit, Stand, Lie 180
First Line, Last Line 182
Fish Bowl 184
Puppets 186
Who? What? Where? 188
The Walls Have Ears 190
New Choice 192
Prompts 194
Silent Scenes 196
All of Me 198
Writer's Raffle 200
What's so Funny? 202
Emotional Baggage 203

Appendices
First and Last Lines 205
Introduction 206
Lines 207
List of locations
Introduction 210
Locations 211

Foreword

Secondary teachers, today more than ever, feel pressed by time, space, and curricular constraints, especially with the focus on high-stakes, nation-wide assessment. When faced with these pressures one of the first things to fall by the wayside is creativity.

Mark Labrow's *Creative Activities for the Secondary Classroom* offers the opportunity to rediscover spontaneity. These highly innovative exercises present teachers and their secondary students with opportunities for collaboration, creativity and critical thinking, all so key to twenty-first-century learning. I would argue that creative education is central to Mark's work, and his emphasis is on helping to draw out students' language, to press on their abilities to articulate their thinking.

But if students are going to grow into increasingly sophisticated language structures, they must have these structures modelled for them, as well as practise, both individually and in collaboration with others. Through Mark's ingenious exercises, students practise many of the actual, linguistic requirements of a strong academic curriculum. They learn to compare and contrast, use hypothetical language, pose and answer questions of substance, utilise sophisticated vocabulary, analyse character and theme, learn about narrative structure, experience ensemble and grow through critique as they weigh the pros and cons of each of their creative decisions. He also blends in ample opportunities for writing; and the mix of talk, drama and writing allows students to consider how best to express themselves in each of these modes.

I've been researching actors, directors and dramatic engagement in students for 20 years, and Mark Labrow is at the top of the list in terms of talent. Smart, funny and full of ideas, he knows exactly how to stretch the language and creative skills of children, adolescents and adults, especially teachers. Having had the privilege of researching Mark's work with a variety of age groups over several years, I can attest to the power of the exercises he provides here.

If, as a teacher, you're interested in learning more about creative teaching and engaging your secondary students in vibrant, dramatic and, most important, *thoughtful*, *cognitively challenging* activities, then this is the book for you.

Dr Shelby A. Wolf
Professor and President's Teaching Scholar
University of Colorado at Boulder

Introduction

This book is a toolbox of games and exercises that can be used in the classroom to enhance engagement and learning. It is written in response to 15 years of practice and experimentation in formal and informal education settings, working with young people aged 5–25.

A high percentage of the teachers and educationalists I have come into contact with during this time have asked for a simple, accessible and, above all, effective instruction manual for creative teaching. I have explored and road-tested drama and theatre conventions in the classroom and utilised them to underpin the curriculum and improve young people's capacity for creativity. The aim of this book and my work in particular, is to explore creativity, spontaneity and play and to find ways of harnessing these skills to enhance the work carried out in the classroom.

Facilitating creativity in others is challenging. Drama is often seen as a fringe subject in our schools, something fun, a welcome distraction from the real work and not really a viable career option. This book is more than just a list of exercises aimed at making young people better actors or supporting the creation of the school play. Through this book I aim to offer practical, easy-to-use exercises that teachers can utilise with their pupils to help them adapt to the rapidly changing world in which they are growing up.

The traditional idea of intelligence is shifting fast. It is no longer only beneficial to have a good memory, retain things that have been taught to us and regurgitate these facts in an end-of-year exam. The world of work is now more demanding than ever. The real commodity in the workplace is ideas. Intellectual property is big business.

Recent developments in the field of multiple and emotional intelligence tell us that to be successful we are required to develop more than just our memory. In today's workplace we need, now more than ever, to excel at working as a member of a team, to be competent in the art of negotiation, have an awareness of ourselves and others, be flexible in our thinking, spontaneous in generating unique ideas and imaginative and creative when it comes to dreaming up solutions to our everyday problems.

The exercises in this book have been selected to help young people develop all of these potentially successful traits and provide teachers with new ways of making lessons come to life.

Although the majority of these exercises come from the world of theatre, their uses are multifaceted. Please don't be afraid to experiment with some of these exercises in other subject areas, you may be surprised to find that they can invigorate and inspire students across the whole curriculum.

You may recognise some of these games and exercises from elsewhere, in fact you may have played many of them yourself. I've learnt many of the exercises from other people and have developed my own slant on most of them. I would like to take this opportunity, however, to thank all the theatre practitioners I worked with, who have shared their knowledge and experience with me and who have shaped my drama practice.

Please feel free to adapt, refine and experiment with these exercises in the hope that they might engage, educate and invigorate your students.

How to use this book

The exercises contained in this book have been broken down under relevant headings. I have made no attempt to link these exercises directly to the curriculum. In my experience, teachers have a far better understanding of what will work in their particular subject area than I have. Even though, at first glance, the exercises seem to be relevant only for Drama or English lessons I have used these successfully to explore History, Geography and Science objectives within the classroom. You'll notice that all the exercises are suitable for KS3 and KS4. This is a deliberate choice. I have used most of these exercises in primary classrooms, secondary schools and with teachers and business leaders. The exercises are ultimately flexible; needing only the slightest adjustment to make them appropriate for a particular age group.

The book is split into the following four chapters which, for drama purposes, lead seamlessly into each other.

Developing a Sense of Team. These exercises are icebreakers, useful when working with a new class or to integrate new members into a group. Developing a team is the first stage of any successful group work. Finding ways to get a group to gel can be difficult, hopefully this chapter provides enough exercises to break down initial inhibitions and to create a feeling of trust within the group.

Developing Focus and Concentration. These exercises are the next stage of group development. All the exercises in this chapter develop speed of thought and an awareness of others. In order to work successfully, a group should be able to direct their focus to the task in hand, these exercises will enhance that skill.

Developing Spontaneity. Building on the previous chapter, 'Developing Spontaneity' takes the notion of quick thinking and begins to move the work into creation. These exercises are all about generating ideas, freeing participants from blocks and developing a sense of playfulness.

Developing Scenes and Stories. In the final chapter students can improvise scenes or use these structures to generate scripts and stories based on a given starting point. This chapter is designed to lead on from the previous chapter, providing an opportunity for students to develop the skill of creative writing.

The book is designed to either be used as a system, with each chapter leading into the next, or for teachers to dip into when looking for inspiration or a quick 'brain game' to wake up and invigorate a class. However you choose to use it, I hope that the exercises add something different to your lessons and that they open up a new way of working for both you and your students.

Acknowledgements

The true source of most exercises is hard to trace, as the origins of games are often blurred. I have attempted to acknowledge all the practitioners and companies with whom I have worked personally and some whose books have been an inspiration and from whom I have learnt so much. Thank you.

Franki Anderson, Mick Barnfather, Ken Campbell, Angela de Castro, Guy Dartnell, Simon Edwards, Phillipe Gaulier, Tony Goode, Jos Houben, Chris Johnston, Keith Johnstone, Marian Masoliver, Jonothan Neelands, Thomas Prattki, Sue Reddish, Viola Spolin, The Suggestibles, Theatre Cap a Pie, John Wright.

To my wife and my parents for all the love, support, belief and happiness they have brought my way.

Chapter 1
Developing a Sense of Team

Introduction

Building an effective team can be challenging; a difficult balancing act. The exercises in this chapter will allow students to understand the importance of working together. Through these team exercises, the group will experience true communication both verbal and non-verbal. The aim is to tune in, to start working as a whole instead of standing alone as an individual. Don't mistake this as trying to make everyone the same, far from it. We want the group to celebrate their differences, but in these exercises they are asked to give and take, to listen to the needs of the group as a whole and to support each of the team members. Teamwork is one of the most important skills, not only in the classroom but also in the workplace. The ability to work together to achieve an agreed goal can sometimes be challenging.

The exercises in this chapter cover a wide range of team building requirements including icebreakers, name games, problem solving exercises and developing trust within the group. Feeling safe and secure with the people you work with on a daily basis is one of the fundamental building blocks of working effectively in any group.

Name Me Thrice

Name Me Thrice is a great icebreaker particularly useful for new groups. The group can develop concentration and focus and learn everybody's name in the process.

Suitable for

KS3, KS4

Aims

- To learn the names of group members.
- To develop speed of thought and quick responses.
- To enhance concentration.

Resources

- None

Space

- Suitable for use in the classroom

What to do

1. Ask the group to stand in a circle with one volunteer in the centre.
2. The aim of the game is for the person in the centre of the circle to say the name of someone standing in the circle three times before that person can say their own name once.
3. If the person in the centre is successful, they swap with whoever was caught out.
4. If they are unsuccessful, they stay in the centre and try again.

Name Tag

Name Tag is an energetic and lively way of waking up a group. This exercise encourages the learning of names whilst increasing focus and spatial awareness.

Suitable for

KS3, KS4

Aims

- To learn the names of group members.
- To develop speed of thought and quick responses.
- To enhance concentration.
- To enhance spatial awareness.

Resources

- None

Space

- Large empty space

What to do

1. The group spread out across the room and someone volunteers to be 'it'.
2. The person who is 'it' must try to tag someone else in the room (as in a normal game of tag).
3. Just before someone is 'tagged' they can call out the name of somebody else in the room. The person who is named suddenly becomes 'it' and can then tag anyone in the room.

Variation

- If this is proving too easy in a large room why not restrict the area of the space and play it in more confined surroundings.

Amazing Adjective Action Names

Amazing Adjective Action Names is a fantastic way to introduce a new group to each other. This exercise gives participants a visual reference point when attempting to remember names.

Suitable for

KS3, KS4

Aims

- To learn the names of group members.
- To develop speed of thought and quick responses.
- To enhance concentration.

Resources

- None

Space

- Suitable for use in the classroom

What to do

1. The group stand in a circle and one person is selected to begin (it's sometimes easier as the facilitator to start this exercise yourself).
2. The first person selected should find an adjective that starts with the same letter of their name and say both the adjective and their name together out loud, e.g. 'Tired Tim'. Tim will also perform a movement that goes along with their adjective, e.g. a yawn.
3. Everyone else in the group repeats 'Tired Tim' and performs his action before the focus shifts to the next person in line.
4. After the second person, the group copy their name and movement and also repeat Tim's name and action.
5. This continues round the circle until everyone has said their name and performed an action. After the last person, obviously the group have to go back through everyone else until they end with Tim.

Know Your Place

Know Your Place is a quick exercise through which individuals can learn more about other members of the group and get a visual representation of the differences and similarities within the team.

Suitable for

KS3, KS4

Aims

- To develop speed of thought.
- To promote understanding of the group.
- To develop interaction and negotiation skills.

Resources

- None

Space

- Suitable for use in the classroom

What to do

1. This exercise is used primarily as an introductory activity or icebreaker for a group.
2. Ask the group to form lines based on individual features such as height, hand size, date of birth, alphabetic order of surnames, shoe size etc. This requires people to interact and negotiate their position in the line up.

Variations

- Give the group a time limit, say thirty seconds or a minute, to position themselves in the line adding to the speed of the game.
- Alternatively get the group to complete the exercise in silence before asking them to rearrange themselves into the correct order.

Cat and Mouse

> Cat and Mouse is a high energy game of 'tag' that calls for quick thinking. Players shift rapidly from cat to mouse and back again calling for concentration and awareness from everyone involved.

Suitable for

KS3, KS4

Aims

- To develop speed of thought and quick responses.
- To enhance concentration.
- To enhance spatial awareness.

Resources

- None

Space

- Large empty space

What to do

1. The 'cat' (tagger) chases the 'mouse'.
2. Everyone else in the group stands in pairs, hands on hips, arms linked and spread around the room.
3. The 'mouse' can escape the 'cat' by linking onto one of the pairs, but by doing so they release a new 'mouse'.
4. Whoever the 'mouse' links, the person at the other end of the pair is released and becomes the 'mouse'.
5. If the 'cat' catches and tags any 'mouse' the 'mouse' instantly becomes the 'cat' and the tables are turned.

Air Ball

Air Ball is a great game for promoting concentration, co-ordination and co-operation. This exercise shows on a practical level how the team operates. You can see the leaders, the people who put themselves forward, the people who find it difficult to share and the people in the group who shy away from responsibility or prefer to take a back seat.

Suitable for

KS3, KS4

Aims

- To develop co-ordination.
- To heighten concentration.
- To encourage teamwork.

Resources

- Sponge football

Space

- Large empty space (with a high ceiling)

What to do

1. Stand the group in a circle and ask one volunteer to start by hitting the ball into the air.
2. The ball must be kept in the air using hands or any part of the body necessary, but no one can hit the ball more than once in a row.
3. Get the group to count out loud, together and see how far the group can get.
4. This game can be extremely addictive and once the group build their confidence, high scores can be achieved.

Bucket Ball

Bucket Ball shows on a practical level how the team operates. You can see the leaders, the people who put themselves forward, the people who find it difficult to share and the people in the group who shy away from responsibility or prefer to take a back seat. The key to Bucket Ball is teamwork and co-operation.

Suitable for

KS3, KS4

Aims

- To encourage teamwork.
- To develop co-ordination.
- To heighten concentration.

Resources

- Sponge football
- Chair
- Bucket

Space

- Large empty space (with a high ceiling)

What to do

1. At one end of the room there is a chair with a bucket sitting on it. The group start from the same end of the room as the chair and bucket.

2. One person hits the ball into the air. The ball must be kept in the air using hands, but no one can hit the ball more than once in a row. The group attempt to move the ball the whole length of the room with everyone in the group touching the ball at least once on its journey to the other end.

3. When everyone has touched the ball and they have reached the far end of the room someone must bounce the ball off the wall and the group make the return journey back to where they started (again on the return everyone should touch the ball).

4. Once back where they started the group must guide the ball into the bucket sitting on the chair.

Variation

- If this exercise proves too difficult, try it with a balloon and then progress to a ball once the group have mastered it.

5 4 3 2 1

5 4 3 2 1 is an excellent ball game requiring co-ordination and concentration. This is one exercise that will take time to master and as such should be practised regularly. This is a real challenge, requiring a high level of teamwork.

Suitable for

KS3, KS4

Aims

- To develop speed of thought.
- To heighten focus and concentration.
- To develop co-ordination and spatial awareness.

Resources

- Sponge football

Space

- Large empty space (with a high ceiling)

What to do

1. This is a variation on the more common game 'Air Ball'.
2. Stand the group in a circle and ask one volunteer to start by hitting the ball into the air. The ball must be kept in the air using hands, with only one person at a time allowed to hit the ball.
3. On the fifth hit of the ball the ball must be struck with another part of the body other than the hand (head, shoulder, knee, foot).
4. The ball remains in play and the game continues using hands to strike the ball but the counting goes back to one.
5. Each hit of the ball is counted until the group reach four, the fourth hit must again be with another part of the body.

6. Counting starts again at one and the on the third hit a different part of the body is used. This continues until the group get down to one.

7. This game takes a long time to master and some groups may become frustrated. The challenge is to work together, concentrate and support each other throughout the exercise.

Variation

- If the group do manage to achieve it and build up a high level of skill at the exercise then ask them to loop the game so once it's completed it continues by going back to the beginning. See how many times they can complete the cycle.

Triangle Tag

> Triangle Tag is an energetic warm up that requires team mates to protect their colleagues. Patience, resilience and strategic thinking are required if the 'tagger' is to get their target and win the game.

Suitable for

KS3, KS4

Aims

- To encourage teamwork.
- To promote strategic thinking.
- To develop co-ordination and spatial awareness.

Resources

- None

Space

- Large empty space

What to do

1. Split the group into teams of four and ask each person to give themselves a letter A, B, C and D.

2. A steps out of the group and B, C and D all join hands to form a triangle.

3. A must then attempt to tag B on the back, whilst C and D try to protect their colleague. A can only go around to tag B, never through arms or under legs.

4. Give each tagger a time limit to achieve their goal. After the designated time limit or once A has been successful B then steps out of the group and attempts to tag C and so on.

Shuffle Monster

> Shuffle Monster is a hilarious exercise designed to promote strategic thinking and problem solving in the group. It requires true teamwork and a cool head to keep the Shuffle Monster away from the empty chair.

Suitable for

KS3, KS4

Aims

- To encourage teamwork.
- To experiment with problem solving techniques.
- To develop spatial awareness.
- To enhance non-verbal communication.

Resources

- Chairs

Space

- Large empty space (allowing people to move comfortably between chairs)

What to do

1. Spread the chairs out around the room roughly an equal distance apart and make sure someone is sitting in every chair.
2. Choose one person and ask them to stand. Take them to the other side of the room (away from their chair).
3. The aim is for the person standing to make their way back to their own chair, however, there is a catch. The person standing can only shuffle back to their chair, knees together, feet apart, almost like a waddling penguin.

4. Before heading back to their chair they declare out loud 'I am the Shuffle Monster and I love to shuffle' (this is usually spoken in a foreign accent, French works well).

5. Everyone else in the room is allowed to move normally and it is their job to stop the person standing (the Shuffle Monster) from sitting back in their chair. This is done by filling it (sitting in it) just before they reach it.

6. As you may have realised this leaves another chair in the room free which the Shuffle Monster heads towards before it is filled by another member of the group.

7. The game sounds as though the Shuffle Monster will be on their feet for ages but this is rarely the case. Try it and watch the group struggle to protect the one empty chair.

Variation

- You can also impose only non-verbal communication between members of the group to make their task even more difficult.

Fill My Chair

Fill My Chair is a variation on Shuffle Monster (see previous page). This is useful when working with a smaller group or when working in limited space.

Suitable for

KS3, KS4

Aims

- To encourage teamwork.
- To experiment with problem solving techniques.
- To develop spatial awareness.
- To enhance non-verbal communication.

Resources

- Chairs

Space

- Suitable for use in the classroom

What to do

1. Set out four chairs in a square formation and ask for volunteers to sit in them.
2. Choose one person to stand in the centre of the square.
3. The people sitting in the chairs must swap places and the person in the centre attempts to sit in one of the chairs as soon as they are vacated. Only nonverbal communication is allowed between the people sitting in the chairs.
4. This game can also be played with more chairs and players. There should always be a reasonable distance between the chairs to allow the person in the centre enough opportunity to steal one of the seats.

Cross-fire

Cross-fire is an excellent warm up, encouraging communication, awareness and high energy. You'll need eyes in the back of your head for this one.

Suitable for

KS3, KS4

Aims

- To encourage teamwork.
- To develop non-verbal communication.
- To sharpen concentration.

Resources

- None

Space

- Suitable for use in the classroom

What to do

1. This exercise can be played by the whole group.

2. Stand everyone in a circle with a volunteer standing in the centre. The people in the circle must swap places with someone else in the group. This is done by making eye contact and making a non-verbal agreement.

3. Once two people have (silently) agreed to swap they make their move. The person in the centre waits for someone in the circle to move. As soon as a gap appears in the circle the person in the middle can take it. The person without a place stays in the middle and the game continues.

4. Once the group get the hang of this game more than one pair can move. Played with a large group this can be lively and energetic, but always remember – before someone moves they must have someone to swap with.

Negotiate

> Negotiate requires great non-verbal communication skills
> and an awareness of others. This exercise highlights just how
> difficult it can be to achieve the simplest task when working as
> part of a larger group.

Suitable for

KS3, KS4

Aims

- To encourage teamwork.
- To develop non-verbal communication.
- To encourage strategic thinking.
- To sharpen concentration.

Resources

- Chairs

Space

- Suitable for use in the classroom

What to do

1. The group sit on chairs, in a circle, facing in, so everyone can see everybody else in the room (this calls for a pretty perfect circle).
2. The aim of the game is to sit next to a person of your choice. Look around the room and select somebody you would like to sit next to (but **don't** make it obvious or say it out loud). This should be a secret selection so that only you know the object of your desire.
3. The way people move is by silent negotiation, making eye contact with somebody else in the room and agreeing with a nod, their authorisation

to swap seats. Once this SILENT negotiation has been made the two people swap chairs.

4. In order to aid communication strictly by eye contact, I sometimes ask group members to sit on their hands, it discourages waving or other signals to attract individuals' attention.

5. Give the group a time limit and count down to the end of the game. Once finished ask everyone to reflect on how well they did and how close they got to their object of desire.

Variation

- As an additional challenge, if people find the original task too easy, ask people to select someone to sit opposite as well as someone to sit next to.

Rules of Engagement

Rules of Engagement requires participants to read the clues given by the group to discover the secret rules they are playing by. This exercise requires players to watch, listen and read the group, sharpening their sense of awareness and focus.

Suitable for

KS3, KS4

Aims

- To develop an awareness of body language.
- To refine the art of questioning.

Resources

- None

Space

- Suitable for use in the classroom

What to do

1. Get the group in a circle and send one member out of the room while the rest choose a rule, e.g. all girls tell the truth and all boys lie or everyone must touch their face before answering.

2. When the person returns, their job is to discover what the rule is by asking questions of individuals in the group about themselves (questions should not be linked directly to the rule).

3. Rules can be hard or simple depending on the age and experience of the group members.

Machines

Machines are created physically by the group with everyone adding to the overall effect. The final machine is a real team effort, helping to develop rhythm, stamina and awareness within the group.

Suitable for

KS3, KS4

Aims

- To develop teamwork.
- To heighten focus and concentration.
- To enhance co-ordination and spatial awareness.

Resources

- None

Space

- Suitable for use in the classroom

What to do

1. This exercise is suitable for the whole group.

2. Get the group in a circle and ask a volunteer to go into the centre and start the 'machine'. The volunteer makes a repetitive movement and sound that can be maintained for a long period (this is important as the first person will be there for some time).

3. The first person sets the rhythm and tempo for the rest of the group. One by one other members of the group enter the circle and add to the 'machine'.

4. Every new person who joins should attempt to find a movement and sound that links or compliments what has already been created. The rhythm and tempo of the 'machine' should always be maintained.

5. Once the 'machine' is in full flow (with at least 10 people as part of it) try speeding it up or slowing it down, and have the group adapt their tempo accordingly. To end the exercise, slow the 'machine' right down until it shuts down altogether.

Variation

- Try giving the group a theme for their machine, e.g. a fear machine, or the machine of friendship. The group must select sounds and movements that convey the theme selected.

Own Goal

Own Goal is a great team exercise calling for ball control, quick responses and excellent goal-keeping skills.

Suitable for

KS3, KS4

Aims

- To develop teamwork.
- To heighten focus and concentration.
- To enhance co-ordination.

Resources

- Sponge football

Space

- Large empty space

What to do

1. The group stand in a circle facing out, legs apart and feet interlinked with the person next to them. Everyone must have hands on their knees and be looking under their legs.

2. One person stands in the centre.

3. The person in the centre rolls or kicks the ball and attempts to get the ball through somebody's legs and out of the circle.

4. Everyone else tries to prevent the ball leaving the circle. If the ball does leave the circle the person who allowed the ball to escape swaps places with the person in the middle and the game continues.

Variation

- This game can also be played in the same formation, but with people in the circle throwing the ball under their legs and attempting to hit the person in the centre. Whoever is successful at hitting the person in the middle swaps places with them.

Agree–Disagree Continuum

> The Agree–Disagree Continuum is a great way to get to know a new group and the values and beliefs that people hold.

Suitable for

KS3, KS4

Aims

- To develop thinking skills.
- To encourage individual decision making.
- To debate values and beliefs held by the group.

Resources

- Agree, Disagree, Don't Know cards

Space

- Suitable for use in the classroom

What to do

1. Place the 'Agree' and 'Disagree' cards on the floor at either end of the room with the 'Don't Know' card in the middle.
2. Tell the group you are going to read a series of statements. If they agree with the statement you read they must go and stand at the 'Agree' side of the room. If they disagree they stand next to the 'Disagree' card. If they are unsure of their opinion they stand in the middle, next to the 'Don't Know' card.
3. Ask them to respond honestly, not just giving the same answers as the crowd or their friends. You can even ask people to justify their responses or attempt to convince others to change their minds.

The Flock

The Flock is a whole group exercise designed to encourage the team to behave as a single entity. Every movement made is copied by the group making it hard to identify the group leader.

Suitable for

KS3, KS4

Aims

- To develop teamwork and co-operation.
- To enhance co-ordination and spatial awareness.

Resources

- None

Space

- Suitable for use in the classroom

What to do

1. Arrange the group in a diamond formation.
2. Choose a leader from one of the four points of the diamond.
3. The leader will perform a series of abstract, slow, clear moves on the spot that the rest of the group will attempt to copy precisely. This continues until the leader turns to their right.
4. When this happens everyone must follow and a new leader takes over the movements (the person at the new point of the diamond).
5. When this person turns to their right, the group again has a new leader. This continues until all four points of the diamond have experienced leading the group.
6. The aim is to make the moves as fluid as possible and for the whole group to move in time with each other and behave as a single entity.

Balancing the Stage

Balancing the Stage helps to develop sensitivity between participants and encourages the use of the whole stage. This exercise can also be used as a structure when creating or blocking scenes.

Suitable for

KS3, KS4

Aims

- To develop teamwork.
- To heighten focus and concentration.
- To enhance co-ordination and fluidity of movement.

Resources

- None

Space

- Empty space

What to do

1. Ask for volunteers to stand in four corners of an imaginary square. This is your stage.

2. Imagine that the stage stands on a central point or pivot suspended off the ground, which means whenever anyone steps onto the stage it tilts. The aim is to keep the stage 'balanced' at all times. As soon as someone steps onto the stage the person in the opposite corner must mirror any movements. If person 'A' walks closer to the centre of the stage person 'B' must also get closer.

3. Once the basic principles have been mastered more people can be introduced to the game.

4. The real challenge then becomes focusing on your partner and continuing to mirror their movements without being distracted by others.

Variation

- Try using this exercise as the basis for a scene. This will ensure that each move is necessary and justified. If four people are onstage the stage must be perfectly balanced throughout. If you're working with an odd number relax the rules slightly, but still attempt to balance up the stage wherever possible.

Verbal Artist

Verbal Artist encourages participants to give clear, direct verbal instructions to help their partner create a physical image.

Suitable for

KS3, KS4

Aims

- To develop teamwork.
- To enhance language skills.
- To develop co-ordination.

Resources

- None

Space

- Suitable for use in the classroom

What to do

1. Ask the class to split into groups of three.
2. Each person in the group chooses to be the artist, the model or the clay.
3. The clay faces the artist. The model stands behind the clay so that the model can be seen by the artist but not by the clay.
4. The model throws a shape and holds it perfectly still. The artist must now describe the shape to the clay and the clay must mould themselves into the required position.
5. The artist cannot mimic the model or physically move the clay into position. The artist can only work verbally.

Variation

If the group get good at this, give the artist a time limit to complete their art work.

Mirrors

Mirrors is a classic drama training exercise that requires participants to move in sync with each other, making it difficult to tell who is leading and who is following.

Suitable for

KS3, KS4

Aims

- To develop teamwork and co-operation.
- To enhance spatial awareness.

Resources

- None

Space

- Suitable for use in the classroom

What to do

1. Ask the group to split in pairs.

2. Spread the pairs equally throughout the space and ask the partners to face each other an arm's length apart and label each other A and B.

3. The As initiate a movement and the Bs mirror exactly what they see. Ask the As to progress slowly at first and stress that it's not a competition to catch each other out. In fact, the most successful pairings are the ones who are most in sync.

4. Once mastered, the As can begin to make their moves more complex and detailed whilst still making it possible for the Bs to mirror precisely.

5. Once the As have led for a period, swap over and allow the Bs to take the lead. Once the pairs become accomplished at this exercise ask them to switch leaders seamlessly during the exercise.

Variations

- There are many variations on the standard mirror exercise (see following pages for more examples).

Mirrors – Guess Who?

Guess Who? is a variation on the classic Mirrors exercise. Participants try to make movements as seamless as possible while a guesser tries to work out who is leading the action.

Suitable for

KS3, KS4

Aims

- To develop teamwork and co-operation.
- To enhance spatial awareness.

Resources

- None

Space

- Suitable for use in the classroom

Here are some strategies that make this game more difficult for the guesser.

What to do

1. Stand the group in a circle. Choose one person as the leader and practise the mirror exercise with everyone in the circle copying the moves of the leader. Try to make the movements as precise and seamless as possible.

2. Once the group become accomplished at this, choose someone in the group to turn their back or close their eyes. Select someone in the circle to be the leader and ask that person to start their movements, instructing the rest of the group to copy.

3. Now let the guesser turn round or open their eyes. Their job is to identify who in the group is leading the movements. Give the guesser three guesses. If in that time they haven't identified the leader the group win. Somebody new is selected as the guesser and the process is repeated.

Tip

Don't all focus on the leader. This game is most successful when participants use their peripheral vision. People in the circle don't necessarily need to look directly at the leader; they could mirror someone else in the group. This means the leader cannot be identified by the eye line of the other players.

Tip

Make sure the leader is looking at someone. The leader is the only person in the circle who is not compelled to look at someone else but this can be a real give away. If the leader's eyes wander or are focused away from the group the guesser can easily pick them out.

Tip

Make all the movements silent. Any audible movement (such as clapping, snapping or slapping) will give the leader away. Noise will produce a canon effect and it will be easy for the guesser to identify the source of the sound.

Mirrors - Whisper on the Wind

Whisper on the Wind is a variation on the classic Mirrors exercise. Participants pass on a simple movement sequence and attempt to keep it the same as it moves through the group.

Suitable for

KS3, KS4

Aims

- To develop teamwork and co-operation.
- To enhance spatial awareness.

Resources

- None

Space

- Suitable for use in the classroom

What to do

1. Ask the group to stand in a straight line with their back to the facilitator (facing away). Tap the end person in the line on the shoulder and get them to turn around to face you. Show them a simple movement sequence using only your hands.

2. Ask the person facing you to mirror the movement sequence as you do it. Only the person looking at you can see this because everyone else in the group is still facing away.

3. Once the person has seen your sequence get them to turn to the person next to them, tap them on the shoulder and pass the movement on.

4. This continues until the movement sequence has travelled all the way down the line to the end. Compare the differences (if any) from the original.

5. This is a good way to enhance the non-verbal communication skills of a group. It may take some time but the aim is to get the group communicating precisely.

Variation

- This exercise can also be played with the group spread randomly around the room. Individuals can stand anywhere in the room but each person must continue to focus on the person they mirrored when standing in the line, positioning themselves in such a way that their vision is not obscured.

    When this exercise works, the effect is a group canon with a wave of movement flowing around the room with no apparent leader.

Mirrors – House of Fun

House of Fun is a variation on the classic Mirrors exercise. Participants echo and extend their partners actions resulting in a weird and distorted version of what they see.

Suitable for

KS3, KS4

Aims

- To develop focus and concentration.
- To encourage spontaneity.

Resources

- None

Space

- Suitable for use in the classroom

What to do

1. Ask people to work in pairs for this exercise. This should be set up in exactly the same way as the traditional mirror exercise, this time, however, the person who is mirroring their partner's movement should find some way to distort what they do (like the mirrors in the old fashioned fun house).

2. A movement can be distorted in whatever way 'feels' right, in this exercise there is no right or wrong. If the group struggle to invent creative responses, you can offer guidance and ask them to respond to movements in the following ways:

   - make a movement bigger or smaller

- make a movement longer or shorter
- make a movement faster or slower
- invert the movement and respond with the opposite side of the body
- copy a movement twice or three times, rather like a canon
- caricature a movement
- reverse a movement.

3. The aim is for the person following to play and experiment with their response to the given movement.

Variation

- Again, this exercise can also be played with the group spread randomly around the room (as in the previous exercise). Individuals can stand anywhere in the room but each person must continue to focus on the person they mirrored when standing in the line, positioning themselves in such a way so that their vision is not obscured.

  This can lead to a bizarre flow of random impulses that pass around the room. This works extremely well as a warm up to increase concentration whilst also breaking down inhibitions and encouraging spontaneity.

Appliances

Appliances, a great team exercise encouraging groups to work instinctively to create physical shapes and to develop spontaneity and negotiation skills.

Suitable for

KS3, KS4

Aims

- To develop teamwork and co-operation.
- To encourage spontaneity.
- To enhance spatial awareness.

Resources

- None

Space

- Suitable for use in the classroom

What to do

1. Split the class into small groups of around 4/5.

2. The workshop leader calls out appliances or shapes for the groups to create, which should be created physically in 3 dimensions (i.e. not just lying on the floor) wherever possible.

3. Everyone in the group (all 4/5) must be in the shape/appliance. Give the group a limited amount of time to complete their shape to encourage quick thinking and rapid decision making.

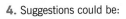

4. Suggestions could be:

- a washing machine
- a sandcastle
- a boat
- a television
- a vacuum cleaner
- an aeroplane
- a settee or chair (which the facilitator must test for stability).

Advertise Me

> Advertise Me is a great way to get to know more about others in the group. Find out as much information as you can and sell, sell, sell.

Suitable for

KS3, KS4

Aims

- To discover more about the group.
- To develop presentation skills.
- To enhance language and vocabulary.

Resources

- None

Space

- Suitable for use in the classroom

What to do

1. Split the group into pairs and give them 5 minutes each to find out as much information about each other as possible. Give them an additional couple of minutes to rehearse a presentation aimed at promoting their partner to the rest of the group.

2. Ask the group to think about the language used in advertising. How can we highlight our partners' good points? This exercise is also about presentation skills. The presentation must be precise, informative and engaging for the audience.

3. Bring the group back together and let each pair go up on stage in an attempt to sell each other to the rest of the group.

Variations

- As an alternative use the premise that the advert is for a dating channel. What qualities does the person have that make them attractive to the opposite sex?
- Try creating an advert for Jobs TV. What different attributes will need to be promoted for a potential employer to take an interest in your partner?

Contract and Expand

Contract and Expand is the ultimate test of non-verbal communication. Can the group behave as one? Can they achieve their goal simply by sensing what others in the group are about to do? This exercise is all about the team.

Suitable for

KS3, KS4

Aims

- To enhance non-verbal communication.
- To develop group awareness.

Resources

- None

Space

- Large empty space

What to do

1. This is an exercise for the whole group.
2. Ask the group to walk around the room with the instruction to walk into any space that they see. This exercise should be done in silence and without communicating with anyone else in the room. The group should not follow any pattern or follow anyone else in the room.
3. Once the group are filling the space equally ask them to continue to walk but to slowly begin to contract into the centre. This should be done over a matter of minutes not seconds.

4. As they begin to slowly contract tell them that when they reach a state of maximum contraction (i.e. when they are as close to each other as they can possibly be and stopped) they should start moving again and begin to slowly expand, taking the group back to how they began (walking freely around the space and filling all the gaps).

5. Have the group experiment with this a few times and get them to loop it so that at the point of full expansion they immediately begin to contract again.

Variation

- Try asking the group (once they've contracted and stopped) to start again one person at a time. Only one person is allowed to move at any one point. If two or three people shuffle or shift their weight the whole group comes back in a clump and the exercise starts again.

Invisible Tug of War

Invisible Tug of War encourages give and take within the group. This exercise shows it's sometimes more fun to play the game than it is to win.

Suitable for

KS3, KS4

Aims

- To be sensitive to others.
- To develop physical co-ordination.

Resources

- None

Space

- Large empty space

What to do

1. This exercise is best played in pairs.
2. Ask a pair of performers to face each other and imagine that they are about to take part in a tug of war. The rest of the group should watch as an audience.
3. The rope they will be using is invisible. Once they pick up the rope they should remain the same distance apart at all times, the rope isn't elastic so shouldn't expand or contract.
4. Ask them both to take their end of the rope in their hands and prepare for battle. Count them in and let the tug of war commence.
5. Observe how they 'play' this game. Is anyone winning? How exciting is the tussle between them? Is the battle going on forever? Is it entertaining the audience?

6. The aim of this exercise is to understand the fundamental principles of teamwork. An important concept in teamwork and, in particular, scene work is the dynamic between two people on stage.

7. Usually this exercise will result in a stalemate with neither performer wanting to lose; they both want to be the best.

8. Ask a few pairs to try it or you could let everyone in the group find a partner and experience what it is like.

9. At the end of this exercise the participants should realise that it's about give and take, not winning. If someone is willing to be beaten or if someone loses right at the last moment it makes for a better scene and for a more dynamic group.

Spell TEAM

Spell TEAM calls for quick thinking, instant reactions and great communication skills. Working against the clock in this exercise really increases the pressure and the team will either pull together or fall apart.

Suitable for

KS3, KS4

Aims

- To improve vocabulary.
- To develop speed of thought.

Resources

- Large sheets of card with the letters of the alphabet written on them

Space

- Large empty space

What to do

1. This exercise is for up to 23 players, but can be played by fewer.
2. Give everyone a letter of the alphabet written on individual pieces of card. Ask the group to stand in alphabetical order (usually it's best to exclude the letters Q, X and Z).
3. The facilitator shouts out words and the group must step forward and rearrange themselves in order to spell out the word required.
4. The words called out should only contain one of each letter, as in the example TEAM (it may be necessary for the facilitator to work out the words in advance).
5. Try working against the clock (10 seconds to create each word), this will really increase the pressure on the group to work together.

Variation

- When you give the group their letters, mix up the order in which they stand so that they are no longer in alphabetical order. This encourages more discussion and negotiation within the team to identify the required letters.

The Game

> The Game proves that you don't have to try too hard to make things happen; sometimes interesting things appear from nowhere. This exercise requires awareness, concentration and the ability to just 'go with the flow'.

Suitable for

KS3, KS4

Aims

- To develop awareness of others.
- To improve non-verbal communication.
- To accept and build on the ideas of others.

Resources

- None

Space

- Large empty space

What to do

1. This exercise can be played by the whole group.
2. Ask the group to stand in a circle. Explain that nobody needs to 'do' anything. Everyone should stand in neutral, hands by their sides, feet together, and do nothing out of the ordinary.
3. At a given signal 'The Game' will begin. The only rules are as follows:
   - No one should make any conscious movement
   - If you see somebody moving (face or body) or making a sound, you must copy what they do.
4. This is 'The Game'. On paper it sounds as though very little should happen, in reality the group will end up giggling together, shaking, jumping around, all manner of movements emanating from very little.

Trust Walk

> Trust Walk is a non-verbal, physical activity that builds awareness and trust between partners and breaks down inhibitions.

Suitable for

KS3, KS4

Aims

- To enhance non-verbal communication.
- To develop trust in others.

Resources

- None

Space

- Large open space with no furniture or obstacles

What to do

1. Ask everyone in the group to find a partner.

2. This is a non-verbal activity and all communication between partners is physical. Ask one partner to close their eyes, and hold out one hand, palm down, in front of them. The other partner places one finger under their palm and guides them around the room.

3. This is a very sensitive exercise and it makes sense to allow the partners to experiment on the spot before they begin to move around the room. Ask the person leading to try to get their partner to go down to the floor or to turn around or to take one step forward and one step back.

4. It will take time for the pairs to 'tune into' each other and this exercise should be given time to develop. When the pairs begin moving around the space ask them not just to walk in circles but to use the whole space.

Variation

- Once everyone is comfortable with the exercise it can be extended further by allowing the leader to let the person with their eyes closed walk, unguided, for brief periods by ceasing physical contact before making contact again and continuing to lead. When the whole group become skilled at this exercise leaders can swap between partners so that they get to guide different individuals and build up awareness and responsibility for everyone in the room.

Trust Circle

Trust Circle is all about supporting members of the team, literally! This exercise takes a great deal of maturity. Done well it can really help to build a sense of togetherness and belonging in a group.

Suitable for

KS3, KS4

Aims

- To enhance non-verbal communication.
- To develop trust in others.

Resources

- None

Space

- Large open space with no furniture or obstacles

What to do

1. Ask the group to split into smaller groups of about 6 or 7 and form a circle.
2. Ask one volunteer from each group to stand in the middle of their circle.
3. The aim is for the person in the centre to close their eyes and keeping their body straight and rigid at all times, lean into the people in the circle.
4. The circle should support the weight of the person in the middle with both hands making sure there are no gaps in the circle. The people in the circle gently pass the volunteer around the circle either side to side or directly across the circle.
5. After a designated time period the group gently bring the volunteer back to an upright, standing position.

Trust Fall

> Trust Fall is similar to Trust Circle but played in pairs. This encourages a sense of real responsibility for each individual in the group.

Suitable for

KS3, KS4

Aims

- To enhance non-verbal communication.
- To develop trust in others.

Resources

- None

Space

- Large open space, free from obstacles

What to do

1. Divide into pairs of students who are approximately the same size.

2. Person A stands with their back to person B. B stands behind A only about a small step away (closer than arm's length). A stands rigid and lets themselves fall gently backwards. B supports A by placing both hands on A's back before returning them to an upright position.

3. Repeat this a few times until both partners are comfortable. Gradually extend the distance between A and B so that A falls slightly further back before receiving support from B.

4. As the distance increases it will become harder and harder to support the weight of A. B should take up a wide, solid stance with one foot slightly further back than the other for maximum strength. It will also be easier if B catches A under the arms as the distance increases between the two.

Variation

- If students are wary about trying the exercise alone then ask them to get into groups of three. Two students can form a cradle by holding onto each other's wrists, while student A stands with their back to the cradle.

  The students behind always give the signal when they are ready by shouting 'fall'. A must always wait for the signal and remain rigid and upright when falling backwards. The catchers take the weight of A and slowly return them to an upright standing position.

Trust Lift

Trust Lift requires the group to work together to raise their volunteer up. This is the ultimate in trust and group confidence. All the volunteer has to do is to relax and enjoy the ride.

Suitable for

KS3, KS4

Aims

- To enhance communication skills.
- To develop trust in others.

Resources

- None

Space

- Large open space, free from obstacles

What to do

1. Ask one volunteer to lie on the floor, arms folded across his chest and body completely rigid. Then ask 8 or 10 other students to lift the volunteer above their heads. Please stress correct lifting procedure (straight back, knees bent).

Object Minefield

In Object Minefield players rely heavily on their partners to communicate effectively and guide them to safety. This is an obstacle course with a difference.

Suitable for

KS3, KS4

Aims

- To enhance communication skills.
- To develop trust in others.
- To problem solve.

Resources

- A scarf or blindfold
- A selection of unbreakable objects (books, chairs, clothing)

Space

- Large open space

What to do

1. The object of this exercise is to help your blindfolded partner to cross a minefield of strategically placed objects safely using only verbal instruction.
2. Ask a volunteer to stand at one side of the room and blindfold them.
3. Give a selected number of the group objects that they can place anywhere in the space, in any configuration (this should be done without talking or prior planning).

4. Select someone to guide the volunteer across the minefield using only verbal directions. The blindfolded volunteer can step or jump over objects if the guide thinks it suitable, but if they touch any object the rest of the group shout 'Boom' and a new volunteer takes their place.

5. This game can be played using a points system. Each time a blindfolded volunteer makes it across the space award 10 points to them and 10 points to their guide. If a blindfolded volunteer hits one of the objects on crossing, award five points to whoever positioned the object/exploded mine. Keep a table and a leader board that is added to each time you play.

Variation

- You can also play the game with more blindfolded volunteers all crossing at the same time. This enhances the noise level and confusion and makes concentration much more difficult, making it a real challenge for the people guiding them across.

The Hand of Hypnosis

The Hand of Hypnosis is an exercise that strengthens non-verbal communication between players. It requires trust and a whole lot of concentration. The 'Hand' can take you anywhere if you let it.

Suitable for

KS3, KS4

Aims

- To enhance non-verbal communication skills.
- To develop trust in others.
- To improve spatial awareness and physical co-ordination.

Resources

- None

Space

- Large open space

What to do

1. The object of this exercise is to develop non-verbal communication between partners in the group.

2. Choose a partner and decide who is A and who is B; A will be 'hypnotised' by B.

3. B holds their hand flat, fingers pointing upwards with their palm a few centimetres away from A's face. A is now 'hypnotised' and must keep their face the same distance away from B's hand for the duration of the exercise.

4. B moves around the space guiding A through a series of positions. A must manipulate their body in any way necessary to maintain the required distance between their face and B's hand.

5. Once the pairs are familiar with this exercise B can swap hands throughout the exercise to challenge A further.

6. B should remember this is a team exercise and their movements should be steady, precise and continuous. After an agreed time period ask the pairs to swap and let A experiment with leading B.

Variation

- Try the same exercise but with the leader using both hands and guiding two people at the same time. The players mustn't touch and it is the responsibility of the leader to keep the players safe throughout the exercise.

Chapter 2
Developing Focus and Concentration

Introduction

The exercises in this chapter are designed to enhance the concentration of the group and improve their ability to think quickly. At times we can all switch off and become de-sensitised to the people around us. These exercises will re-invigorate a group, wake up their senses and allow them to 'tune in' to one another.

Use these exercises at the start of a lesson or first thing in the morning to enhance concentration levels. The classroom is sometimes a difficult place to focus – so many people with so many different needs and agendas. The exercises in this section can be used to 'gel' a group and to engage students at both a physical and cerebral level. To succeed at these exercises requires alertness, awareness and a high level of concentration. What better way to start the day?

1, 2, 3

1, 2, 3 is an excellent brain gym exercise and works both sides of the brain. This is an enjoyable exercise that allows for mistakes and encourages players to persevere till the end.

Suitable for

KS3, KS4

Aims

- To heighten concentration.
- To promote goodwill and eye contact.
- To accept mistakes.

Resources

- None

Space

- Classroom or open space (requires enough room for everyone to work in pairs with space between the pairs).

What to do

1. Ask people to find a partner and face each other (partners should attempt to maintain eye contact throughout the exercise). The aim is to count to three but sequentially, each person taking a turn to speak.

    A – 1, B – 2, A – 3, B – 1, A – 2, B – 3, A – 1, and so on.

2. Once the group have mastered this introduce the next level. This time the number 1 is never said. Instead the number 1 is replaced with an action (a clap, a squat down, a wave or whatever action the facilitator prefers). The same sequence is then repeated, but instead of 1 being said the action is performed. The numbers 2 and 3 are still verbalised.

3. Once the group have had a chance to experience this version, then introduce an action for the number 2. The number 3 is still verbalised. The sequence will then look like this.

A – clap, B – squat down, A – 3, B – clap, A – squat down, B – 3, A – clap.

4. Finally, replace the number 3 with an action until nothing is verbalised and the whole exchange is completely physical.

1 to 20

> 1 to 20 is an exercise designed to encourage the group to work together. It relies on focus, awareness of others and an ability to tune into the group. This is a fantastic exercise to bring the group together and to focus minds.

Suitable for

KS3, KS4

Aims

- To develop focus and concentration.
- To promote teamwork.

Resources

- None

Space

- Suitable for use in the classroom

What to do

1. The group stand in a circle with everyone facing outwards.
2. Ask the group to close their eyes and focus. In order for this exercise to work there needs to be a feeling of calm and whole group concentration.
3. The group are asked to count from 1 up to 20 but with only one person allowed to speak at any one time. There should be no obvious pattern and no pre-conceived plan of who speaks when. If two (or more) people speak at the same time the group must start again.
4. This is a frustrating exercise and takes time and patience to master. Despite its frustrating nature, it's also highly addictive and the group will want to practise over and over to achieve the end result.

Stop – Go

> Stop – Go is an enjoyable, highly addictive exercise that challenges participants' ability to listen, focus and concentrate. When played at speed it can become confusing (which is good) and take some time to master.

Suitable for

KS3, KS4

Aims

- To develop speed of thought.
- To heighten concentration.

Resources

- None

Space

- Large empty space

What to do

1. The group walk around the room with the instruction to walk into any space that they see. This exercise should be done in silence and without communicating with anyone else in the room.

2. The facilitator tells the group to follow two very simple instructions. When they hear 'Stop' the group are to stop. When they hear 'Go' the whole group are to start walking. Simple! Give the group a few opportunities to practise this and encourage them by telling them how good they are at the exercise.

3. Then explain that the rules are about to change slightly. Now when the facilitator says 'Stop' it means 'Go' and when the group hear 'Go' it means 'Stop'. Ask if everyone understands, usually people nod, after all it still sounds pretty simple. Let the group start walking by shouting 'Stop' and then alternate your instructions as the exercise progresses.

If the group get the hang of this introduce the instructions 'Up' (jump in the air) and 'Down' (touch the floor) which they must perform in the same way as 'Stop', 'Go'. This exercise is excellent at promoting focus and concentration and, in addition, is great fun.

Big Booty

Big Booty is a hilarious warm up exercise designed to develop quick thinking and concentration. A classic game, high energy, lots of fun and extremely addictive.

Suitable for

KS3, KS4

Aims

- To develop speed of thought.
- To heighten concentration.

Resources

- None

Space

- Suitable for use in the classroom

What to do

1. Stand the group in a circle. One person is given the title 'Big Booty' and everyone else numbers themselves to the left of 'Big Booty' from number one upwards.

2. The game starts with everyone saying the following; in rhythm (the rhythm is extremely important).

   'Big Booty, big booty, big booty (*beat*), big booty, big booty, oh no.'

   Big Booty then says 'Big Booty, number four.'

   And number four passes it on saying 'Number four, number six.'

   'Number six, number two.'

3. At any point it can be passed back to Big Booty 'Number two, Big Booty.'
'Big Booty, number one.'

4. This continues until someone makes a mistake, stumbling over the words, saying it out of beat or just missing their turn. The person who makes the mistake goes back to number one, standing next to Big Booty and everyone moves up a number. If Big Booty is caught out they go to number one and the person to Big Booty's right fills Big Booty's place.

5. As each person makes a mistake people change numbers, and this is what makes the exercise so difficult, confusing but ultimately so much fun. This is an excellent, high energy warm up that generates laughter and frustration in equal measure.

Yes Torpedo

Yes Torpedo encourages the group to work together, supporting each other, whilst maintaining a state of alertness and awareness of everyone in the room.

Suitable for

KS3, KS4

Aims

- To develop speed of thought.
- To heighten concentration.
- To encourage support of others in the team.

Resources

- None

Space

- Suitable for use in the classroom

What to do

1. Stand the group in a circle and ask one volunteer to begin the game (A).
2. A must make eye contact with someone else in the circle (B). Once eye contact has been established B should then say 'Yes' and A walks across the circle to take up B's position.
3. B must then look at someone else across the circle and make eye contact. Whoever is selected should say 'Yes' and B makes their way across the circle to take their place. The game continues.
4. The aim is for each person to make eye contact, be given permission to move with a 'Yes' and leave their place in the circle before they are hit by the human torpedo (the person they said 'Yes' to, who is heading towards them across the circle).
5. If they fail to move before the torpedo reaches them the whole group shout 'Boom' and the game starts again.

Rag Tail

Rag Tail is a game of strategy, awareness and quick reflexes. Be alert at all times and protect your tail, no player is to be trusted. Remember ... he's behind you!

Suitable for

KS3, KS4

Aims

- To develop spatial awareness.
- To encourage speed of thought and response.

Resources

- Handkerchiefs (ideally coloured)

Space

- Large empty space

What to do

1. Each member of the group is given a handkerchief that they tuck into the back of their trousers.

2. The whole group is then asked to move around the space, eyeing each other up, before the game commences. This heightens anticipation and ups the stakes of the game. On a signal from the facilitator the game begins.

3. The object of the game is to steal as many handkerchiefs as possible without having yours stolen. As soon as your handkerchief is seized you must exit the game.

4. The winner is the person with the most handkerchiefs in their possession at the end.

Catch it – Drop it

Catch it – Drop it is an exercise designed to catch you out. You're told to do one thing but must do the opposite. High levels of concentration and physical awareness are needed to stay in the game.

Suitable for

KS3, KS4

Aims

- To develop co-ordination and speed of thought.
- To heighten concentration.

Resources

- Sponge/tennis ball

Space

- A large enough space where the whole group can stand in a circle

What to do

1. The group stand in a circle with one person in the centre.
2. The person in the centre throws the ball to someone in the circle while calling a command. The command can be 'Catch it' or 'Drop it'. The person who is receiving the ball must do the opposite of the command (i.e. If 'Drop it' is called they must 'Catch it').
3. If they get it wrong they swap places with the person in the centre and the game continues.

Person to Person

Person to Person is a great exercise for mixing up people in the group and breaking down cliques. The exercise also calls for quick reflexes and accurate physical responses.

Suitable for

KS3, KS4

Aims

- To mix up an established group.
- To encourage work with different members of the class.
- To break down physical inhibitions.
- To develop co-ordination and speed of thought.

Resources

- None

Space

- Large empty space

What to do

1. Ask people to find a partner and face each other.
2. The facilitator shouts out body parts that each pair must join together, e.g. elbow to elbow, toe to toe, ear to ear. When the facilitator shouts 'Person to Person' everyone finds a new partner to work with.
3. The facilitator can vary the speed of the instructions to really keep the group on their toes. This can be an excellent way of mixing up a group and breaking down physical inhibitions.

Fuzzy Duck

> Fuzzy Duck is guaranteed to end in hilarity. Fuzzy Duck confuses and baffles and, played at speed, calls for an extremely high level of concentration.

Suitable for

KS3, KS4

Aims

- To develop speed of thought.
- To heighten concentration.

Resources

- None

Space

- Suitable for use in the classroom

What to do

1. Stand the group in a circle and ask for the phrase Fuzzy Duck to be passed, in sequence, around the group.

2. Explain that the direction of Fuzzy Duck can be changed by anyone who says 'Does he?' Upon hearing 'Does he?' the phrase changes to 'Ducky Fuzz' and is sent around the circle in the opposite direction. When 'Does he?' is asked again the direction is again reversed and reverts to 'Fuzzy Duck'. This sequence continues throughout the duration of the game.

3. Whoever stumbles over the words, stalls or swears in this game is out. *(Be aware this game can inadvertently result in players swearing. If this would be an issue please don't use this exercise.)*

Zip, Zap, Boing

In Zip, Zap, Boing players send Zips, Zaps and Boings flying around and across the circle at pace. The aim is to keep the energy up and the game fizzing along without hesitation.

Suitable for

KS3, KS4

Aims

- To develop speed of thought.
- To heighten concentration.

Resources

- None

Space

- Suitable for use in the classroom

What to do

1. Stand the group in a circle.
2. Players pass a Zip, a Zap or a Boing around the circle. Zips can only be passed to your left and this is how the game should begin. The facilitator should start the game by turning to the person on their left, clapping once and saying Zip. This is then passed on in exactly the same way until the Zip has gone once around the circle (the Zip should move at pace, without hesitation).

3. The Zip will continue to move in the same direction (left) and at the same pace until it is blocked by a Boing. To use a Boing a player must perform a star jump and say Boing. This reverses the direction of the Zip and turns the Zip into a Zap. Zaps only move round the circle to your right. So if you pass a Zip to the person on your left and that person performs a Boing you must turn to the person on your right and pass them a Zap, this continues to move round the circle until someone uses a Boing and it reverts to being a Zip.

4. Boing's can also be used to send the energy across the circle. To do this the person using a Boing must make eye contact with someone across the circle before sending them a Boing. The receiving player can then decide to keep the game moving by turning to their left and saying Zip or turning to their right and sending round a Zap or Boinging right back at them.

One Step Back

One Step Back is an excellent exercise that tests participants' memory and concentration. This is a test of recall and the ability to memorise sequences.

Suitable for

KS3, KS4

Aims

- To improve memory and recall.
- To develop focus and concentration.

Resources

- None

Space

- Suitable for use in the classroom

What to do

1. This exercise requires participants to point at objects in the room and give them a completely new name.

2. Ask people to point at an object (any object) in the room and call it a 'Donkey'. Whatever they pointed at and called 'Donkey' (say it was a table) then becomes the name of the next thing they point at. They are naming things one step back (hence the name).

3. Continue to go round the room naming things in this way. Perform this exercise at pace and see how many things people can name in an allotted time.

Variations

- You can challenge the group even more by asking them to stop at any given moment and asking them to point at and recall the objects in reverse order.
- As an added challenge you can ask the group to point at an object and give it a completely new (and unrelated) name. For example if someone points at a wall they say 'Wind', they then point at a door handle and say 'Remote control'.

Prisoner

Prisoner encourages eye contact, physical awareness and communication. Participants must stay alert, be aware of their surroundings and be poised to make a run for it at any time.

Suitable for

KS3, KS4

Aim

- To develop group awareness.
- To enhance eye contact between the group.
- To encourage quick thinking and reflexes.

Resources

- Chairs

Space

- Suitable for use in the classroom

What to do

1. Ask just over half the group to take a chair and place them in a circle in the middle of the room and stand directly behind their chair (these people are the prison guards). The remaining people in the group sit down in any chair in the circle.

2. Now some people should be standing behind chairs with people sitting in front of them and some people will be standing behind empty chairs.

3. If a person standing behind a chair (prison guard) has someone sitting in their chair, the person sitting is their prisoner. Prison guards standing behind the chairs can only communicate with the prisoners sitting in the chairs by winking.

4. If a prisoner is winked at by a prison guard then the prisoner must make their way to the empty chair. However, if the person standing behind them tags them on the shoulder before they have a chance to leave their chair they must remain seated.

5. All prison guards must stand one arm's length away from their chair and can only stop the prisoner escaping by tapping them on the shoulder or back.

6. The aim is for the people standing behind the chairs (prison guards) to have someone sitting in their chair (prisoner) at the end of an agreed time limit.

7. At the end of the game anyone without someone sitting in a chair in front of them must remain standing and everyone else swaps (i.e. the seated people stand and the standing people sit).

Bang!

> Bang! is a quick fire (literally) warm up exercise designed to develop awareness, focus and concentration. Be ready or the sheriff could shoot you down at any time.

Suitable for

KS3, KS4

Aims

- To enhance group awareness.
- To develop co-ordination and concentration.

Resources

- None

Space

- Large empty space

What to do

1. The whole group stand in a circle and one person is chosen to stand in the middle as the 'sheriff'. Everyone puts their hands together as if holding a gun.

2. The 'sheriff' can choose who to 'shoot' which he does by pointing at them with his imaginary gun and shouting 'Bang!'

3. Whoever he points at must duck and the two people either side must turn to shoot each other. Whoever is the slowest (i.e. the last person to say 'Bang') loses and must sit down.

4. The game continues until there are only two people left. The final two stand back to back and take five paces away from each other. They stand, guns poised, facing away from each other until the 'sheriff' gives the order to fire. Whoever is the quickest on the draw wins and becomes the new 'sheriff'.

Sticks

Sticks is the ultimate exercise to develop focus and concentration. Participants tune in to each other as the sticks fly around the room. Not for the faint-hearted.

Suitable for

KS3, KS4

Aims

- To enhance group awareness.
- To develop focus and concentration.
- To work effectively as a group.
- To enhance spatial awareness and co-ordination.

Resources

- Broom handles (× 12)

Space

- Large empty space

What to do

1. First, get the group to stand in a circle facing in with you (the facilitator) in the middle.
2. Take one broom handle and hold it in your hand vertically with your hand just above the midway point, thumb behind. The aim is to throw the stick through the air to another member of the group to catch. As it flies through the air it should remain vertical for them to catch. Once this has been mastered (and they have thrown it back) send it to another person in the group. Repeat this until everyone in the group has caught and thrown the stick successfully.

3. Collect all the sticks together and ask the group to walk around the room filling any gaps on the floors they can see (aim to get an even spread of bodies across the space).

4. Ask them to start making eye contact with people as they pass, but not talking or making any physical contact. The pace should be brisk.

5. Introduce each broom handle into the group by making eye contact with one member.

6. Throw the stick to them and they should attempt to catch the stick and continue moving around the space at the same pace. This broom handle is then thrown to another member of the group in the same way (it must be thrown, not handed). This continues until most of the group have become comfortable moving around the space, throwing and receiving the sticks.

7. Once the group become settled with this rhythm, introduce the second broom handle (and so on until the group have around half as many sticks as there are group members). This exercise quickly builds awareness and concentration; it's surprising how quickly people 'tune' into each other with wooden sticks flying around their ears.

8. As the confidence of the individuals grows, see if they can pass a stick to someone else in the group who already has one. This takes great care and a high level of trust. If anyone does drop a stick (it happens quite regularly to begin with) ask members of the group not to apologise or comment on it. Ask them simply to pick up the stick and continue, rather like they would in a play if they made a mistake with their lines.

Brain Flop

> Brain Flop sounds simple, but it's anything but. This exercise requires high levels of focus, concentration and teamwork to keep the momentum going.

Suitable for

KS3, KS4

Aims

- To develop speed of thought.
- To heighten concentration.

Resources

- None

Space

- Suitable for use in the classroom

What to do

1. This is a concentration game which is played in groups of 5.
2. Ask the group to stand in a circle. The task for the group starts simply. Ask them to count from 1 to 6 with each person saying the next number in the sequence. Let the group go through this sequence two or three times before introducing the first restriction.
3. Once they have mastered the simplicity of counting from 1 to 6 ask the group to replace the number 1 with the word 'brain'. When the group have practised this for a few minutes introduce rule two.
4. Ask the group to replace number 4 with the word 'flop' whilst still saying 'brain' for number 1 (hence the name of the game). Let them practise this and continue to replace the remaining numbers with words until the group are left with only words moving around the circle.

Focus Line Up

Focus Line Up is a classic exercise that demonstrates the power of focus. Once the group have mastered focus, teamwork becomes much easier and communication much more effective.

Suitable for

KS3, KS4

Aims

- To develop focus.
- To heighten concentration.
- To build confidence.

Resources

- None

Space

- Suitable for use in the classroom

What to do

1. This exercise is best played with 5 participants.
2. Ask the participants to stand in a line facing the audience and ask the audience who has the focus. Usually the focus of the audience will wander up and down the line depending on a number of factors. This exercise is about channelling the focus to where we want it to be.
3. Ask the person on the left of the line to continue looking straight out to the audience and all the other participants to turn to look at this person.

4. Check back with the audience now and ask the same question. See if their focus has been drawn to one person in particular. Ask them what draws their attention away from this person.

5. The person who is facing forward (who should have everyone's focus) then turns to face the person next to them. They make eye contact and hold this for a few seconds before the second person in the line turns to face the audience. Everyone in the line should now be looking at person two. This should mean that the focus of the audience is now on this person.

6. After a few minutes of person two holding the focus they turn to person three and the pattern is repeated until the focus shifts all the way down the line to the person on the end.

7. This is a great exercise that can enhance the discipline of other performers on stage and show the audience the importance of focus when working on stage.

Variation

• As well as simply passing the focus along the line try introducing emotions. Start at one end with a little smile and pass it down the line asking each person to exaggerate it slightly until it grows to a raucous laugh when it reaches the end.

Ha!

Ha! is a team exercise requiring the group to become aware of each other, be alert and respond quickly in unison. When done successfully the whole group become one.

Suitable for

KS3, KS4

Aims

- To develop focus.
- To heighten concentration.

Resources

- None

Space

- Suitable for use in the classroom

What to do

This exercise can be played with the whole group.

1. Ask the participants to stand in a circle.

2. Tell the group that at random points you will place your hand in the centre of the circle, hand flat, palm facing down and shout 'Ha'. The aim of the exercise is for everyone else in the circle to 'tune in' and copy your action in perfect synchronisation.

3. This takes some time and most efforts will result in some people being out of sync. As the leader, vary the pace and frequency of your 'Ha'.

4. You may find that everyone fixates on the leader, but this isn't the best way to approach the exercise. Ask the group to all send their focus into the centre of the circle and use their peripheral vision and awareness to sense when the next 'Ha' might be.

Variations

- You can also try this exercise using a clap instead of the 'Ha'. The 'Ha' has more power because of the vocal impact linked to the physical movement, but a clap can work just as well.
- As another alternative you can try this with the group spread out around the room, either static or walking. This is obviously more difficult and requires a great deal of awareness and focus from the group.

The Impulse to Go

The Impulse to Go is an exercise for pairs. This is all about timing, sensitivity and awareness. The skill is to stay visually connected to your partner and find the right moment to go.

Suitable for

KS3, KS4

Aims

- To develop focus.
- To heighten concentration.
- To enhance non-verbal communication.

Resources

- Garden canes or broom handles

Space

- Suitable for use in the classroom

What to do

1. This exercise is played in pairs.
2. Ask the participants to stand facing each other about a metre apart.
3. Each person has a garden cane or stick placing one end on the floor and their finger on top. They make eye contact and look for the moment to 'go'. The moment to 'go' must be found without making a signal (no verbal cue, wink or nod of the head).
4. When the partners feel the moment is right they release their canes, moving to their left so that they don't collide, and try to grab their partner's cane before it falls to the ground.

5. This can be practised a few times at this distance to ensure the pairs are comfortable with the process. Once they grasp the exercise and can achieve it, ask each pair to move slightly further apart.

6. The distance between each member of the pair should continue to grow until the point they can no longer grab their partner's cane in time.

7. It is important that no obvious signal is made. The pairs should 'tune in' and have a sense of when to move. They should begin to close down their awareness of the rest of the room and concentrate solely on their partner and the cane.

Chapter 3
Developing
Spontaneity

Introduction

There is a balance at work between generating ideas, forcing them to come and simply allowing them to emerge through the work. Spontaneity is the art of quick thinking, of not censoring your impulses and generating honest and instantaneous responses. Creativity hinges on an ability to dream up new possibilities and developing spontaneity supports the creative process. To be truly spontaneous, individuals must trust themselves and their ideas without fearing the future and blocking their imagination and impulses.

This chapter is all about getting the young people you work with to take risks, respond spontaneously and generate new ideas. The aim is to have a new generation of thinkers, people who can build on the ideas of others, can see connections between things, even though at first glance they seem unrelated, and can think instinctively, overcoming problems and barriers using their new found ingenuity.

What's in the Box?

What's in the Box is an exercise designed to encourage participants to live in the moment, generate instant ideas and trust their instinct. This exercise is a great warm up, suitable for any lesson.

Suitable for

KS3, KS4

Aims

- To encourage spontaneity and creativity.
- To develop playfulness and imaginative responses.

Resources

- None

Space

- Suitable for use in the classroom

What to do

1. Ask the group to split into pairs and sit down facing each other (this can be on the floor or across tables/desks).

2. One person is 'A' the other is 'B'. Imagine that A and B have a box sitting between them. 'A' reaches into the box and mimes taking out an object. 'B' asks 'What's in the box?' and 'A' replies with the first thing that comes to mind.

3. This sequence is repeated, faster and faster, really testing the ingenuity and spontaneity of player 'A'.

4. After an agreed time limit the pairs swap and it's B's turn to generate a world of weird and wonderful objects.

Alliteration

Alliteration is a simple but effective way to improve the vocabulary of a group and encourage greater spontaneity and responsiveness.

Suitable for

KS3, KS4

Aims

- To encourage spontaneity.
- To extend vocabulary.

Resources

- None

Space

- Suitable for use in the classroom

What to do

1. This exercise can be done in pairs, small groups or as a whole group.
2. Choose a letter from the alphabet and try to come up with as many words beginning with that letter. It warms up the mind and generates far more words than you can think of alone.

Variations

- As an extension to this exercise you can ask the group to write down the words that were said and attempt to incorporate as many as possible into an alliterative sentence (allow 'the, a, it, to, and for' as linking words). 'The gangly goose gave Graham a green go-kart.'

- You could even make this a whole group exercise by writing words on cards and placing them on the floor and asking pupils to build the sentence one word at a time.

Word Association

Word Association works in a similar way to Alliteration. It requires participants to think quickly and is great for extending vocabulary. It should be played at speed to encourage spontaneity and instantaneous responses.

Suitable for

KS3, KS4

Aims

- To encourage spontaneity.
- To extend vocabulary.

Resources

- None

Space

- Suitable for use in the classroom

What to do

1. Ask the group to sit in a circle, either on the floor or on chairs.
2. The facilitator starts the exercise by saying a word, such as "Park". The next person in the circle says a word that has an association with the previous word or follows it logically. For example:

   Facilitator: Park
   Student A: Bench
   Student B: Press
   Student C: Iron
   Student D: Shirt
   Student E: Suit
   Student F: Diamonds.

3. Any association that makes sense is allowed. If someone in the group questions the relevance of a word ask the person who said the word to justify the link.

4. If the student can't think of a word or hesitates for too long they are deemed to be 'out' and are asked to stand up and the game re-commences.

5. The last student to remain seated is the winner.

Rhyme Time

Rhyme Time is another exercise similar to Alliteration. Participants are expected to respond quickly to a given word, their task is made more difficult as their response needs to rhyme.

Suitable for

KS3, KS4

Aims

- To develop spontaneity.
- To extend vocabulary.

Resources

- None

Space

- Suitable for use in the classroom

What to do

1. This exercise works best in groups of 5.

2. Line up 5 people in front of you. Explain that this exercise is all about speed of thought and rhyming.

3. The first person in the line will produce rhymes for as many words you throw at them as possible. Every time they produce a rhyme they stay in pole position, every time they hesitate, stutter or get it wrong they go to the end of the line.

4. This is a quick-fire exercise that calls for speed of thought and spontaneous reaction. You could ask someone to keep score for the individuals if you want to make it more competitive and have a Rhyme Time champion.

Variation

- This exercise can also be played as a whole class with everyone lined up and the teacher firing words to one person at a time. If someone gives a correct answer the focus moves to the next person in the line. If, however, someone gives an incorrect rhyme they must sit out.

Shift

> Shift is a quick-fire, rapid response exercise. It requires the players to think spontaneously and adapt their physical positions in an instant. This is an excellent exercise for breaking down barriers and encouraging freedom of expression.

Suitable for

KS3, KS4

Aims

- To encourage spontaneity.
- To develop playfulness and imaginative responses.
- To break down physical inhibitions.

Resources

- None

Space

- Suitable for use in the classroom

What to do

1. In pairs, one person performs a repetitive action and sound that can be easily maintained.

2. The other partner can say 'shift' at any point during the action and the person performing the routine must change to a completely different movement and sound (without thinking or stopping). Again the partner says 'shift' and the routine is replaced with another movement and sound.

3. As the person saying 'shift', try to vary the amount of time you leave your partner performing their action. Test their ingenuity; leave them for a while in one movement before a series of rapid fire 'shifts' really push them to the limit of spontaneity. This continues until the facilitator decides that the pairs should swap over and the sequence is repeated.

What are you Doing?

What are you Doing is an exercise designed to test the ingenuity of the participants. It's an excellent team exercise, encouraging the acceptance of ideas and rediscovering the ability to play.

Suitable for

KS3, KS4

Aims

- To encourage spontaneity.
- To develop playfulness and imaginative responses.

Resources

- None

Space

- Large empty space

What to do

1. The group stand in a circle and one person volunteers to go into the middle.
2. The volunteer is asked to perform and action (this could be anything from skiing to brushing a dog).
3. One person from the circle enters and asks 'What are you doing?' The person in the circle performing the action must answer with something completely different (e.g. if they are skiing they could say 'I'm bouncing on a trampoline'). Whatever the person in the centre says the person who has entered the circle must perform.
4. The same sequence is repeated until everyone has had a turn.

What the Audience Want

What the Audience Want teaches participants to be more sensitive to the needs of the group. This exercise is about listening to clues, adapting your responses and being creative to achieve the audience's goal.

Suitable for

KS3, KS4

Aims

- To develop sensitivity and awareness.
- To generate imaginative responses.

Resources

- None

Space

- Suitable for use in the classroom

What to do

1. Get the group in a circle and send one volunteer out of the room while the rest choose a task they would like the volunteer to perform. The task could be anything from sitting on a chair or hopping on one leg to singing a line from a song whilst wearing their tie as a headband. Make the task relevant to the age of the group and to their experience of playing this game.

2. Explain to the group that once the volunteer enters the room the only form of communication is clapping. When the volunteer does something relevant to the task, e.g. steps towards the chair or touches his tie the group clap to give encouragement. If he does something irrelevant to the task they stay silent. The closer the volunteer gets to completing the task the louder the clapping gets.

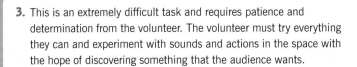

3. This is an extremely difficult task and requires patience and determination from the volunteer. The volunteer must try everything they can and experiment with sounds and actions in the space with the hope of discovering something that the audience wants.

Sound Ball

Sound Ball is great for encouraging spontaneous verbal and physical responses. The great thing is it's about trusting your instinct and very little thought is required. It can sometimes look ridiculous from the outside but that is part of the fun. Get the group to let themselves go and prove that generating ideas can be physical as well as cerebral.

Suitable for

KS3, KS4

Aims

- To develop speed of thought.
- To heighten concentration.
- To enhance communication between team members.

Resources

- None

Space

- Suitable for use in the classroom

What to do

1. Stand the group in a circle and ask one volunteer to begin making a repetitive movement and sounds.

2. The volunteer walks into the centre of the circle and chooses someone else in the group by making eye contact with them.

3. The chosen person mirrors the volunteer in the centre of the circle and copies exactly their noise and movement.

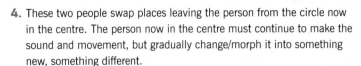

4. These two people swap places leaving the person from the circle now in the centre. The person now in the centre must continue to make the sound and movement, but gradually change/morph it into something new, something different.

5. Once they have discovered a new sound and movement they make eye contact with someone in the circle and repeat the process.

6. This exercise continues until everyone has experienced being in the centre of the circle.

Arms Through

Arms Through requires partners to work closely together and to link speech and movement seamlessly. This exercise develops awareness, teamwork and communication.

Suitable for

KS3, KS4

Aims

- To develop awareness and speed of thought.
- To heighten concentration.
- To enhance teamwork.
- To encourage speaking and listening.

Resources

- None

Space

- Suitable for use in the classroom

What to do

1. This exercise is played in pairs.
2. Ask one person to stand in front of the other with their arms behind their back (A). The person standing behind (B) puts their arms through their partner's so it looks like they are A's arms.
3. Let the pairs experiment with working in such close proximity. Ask B to stroke the chin of A or straighten their tie or roll up their sleeves. Coach them through the opening stages by giving them instructions.

4. Once the pairs are comfortable with this ask one pair to perform to the rest of the group. Give the volunteers a starting point, e.g. a car salesperson trying to sell a car to the rest of the group.

5. This exercise is all about teamwork and spontaneity. It works best when A reads what B's arms are doing and responds accordingly and when B follows the lead of what A is saying and enhancing it physically. They should both create and both respond to how the scene develops.

Variation

- Once a few pairs have experienced performing in front of the group try an Arms Through scene, maybe two teachers in the staffroom or an instructor preparing a student for their first sky dive.

Last Letter

> Last Letter challenges individual responses and calls for quick thinking, co-ordination and concentration. This is an excellent warm up exercise to enliven any group.

Suitable for

KS3, KS4

Aims

- To develop speed of thought.
- To heighten concentration.
- To enhance vocabulary.

Resources

- Tennis ball

Space

- Suitable for use in the classroom

What to do

1. Stand the group in a circle with the teacher/facilitator in the centre.
2. The facilitator throws the ball to someone in the group and says a word (e.g. big).
3. Whoever catches the ball must throw the ball back to the facilitator and reply with a word that begins with the last letter of the word the facilitator said to them (e.g. grape).
4. It is not necessary for there to be an association between the words other than that the last letter of the facilitator's word must be the first letter of the student's word.

5. Once the ball is returned to the facilitator they pass it to someone else in the circle and the game continues.

6. The sequence of words may be something like this:

   Big, grape, echo, outside, even, nothing . . . and so on.

7. Once the group get used to playing this exercise you can have the students throwing to each other.

8. It's important that this is a quick-fire game and that there are no hesitations. If anyone stalls, hesitates or fails to come up with a quick response they're out and are asked to sit down.

Variations

- Try this exercise passing the ball round the circle instead of throwing it. Start the ball going to the left round the circle. If anyone says a word ending in a vowel reverse the direction. Also try putting a block on certain words like 'Apple' or 'Great' to test the mental agility of the group.
- This exercise can also be used to create effective improvised scenes, see '**Last Letter Scenes**'.

I am a Sandwich

I am a Sandwich is an exercise designed to allow a group to develop their ideas one step at a time. It calls for creativity and spontaneity but also requires the ability to listen and work to the needs of the group. This exercise will highlight the real team players in your group.

Suitable for

KS3, KS4

Aims

- To encourage spontaneity.
- To build on the ideas of others.
- To enhance creative thinking.

Resources

- None

Space

- Suitable for use in the classroom

What to do

1. The group stand in a circle. The inside of the circle is the performance space.

2. One person runs into the space, forms their body into a shape or performs a mime that represents to the rest of the group what they are. They then announce to the rest of the group what they are (e.g. 'I am a seat.')

3. Instantly the next person runs on and takes the shape of something else in the picture ('I am a steering wheel.')

4. The next person continues to accept what has gone before and build upon the image being created ('I am a gearstick.')

5. The picture should be added to until whatever is being created is completed in its entirety.

6. At this stage everyone in the image can say in unison the name of the thing they have created ('We are a car.')

7. Played at speed (as it should be) this is an excellent exercise to encourage not only spontaneity but also teamwork. As in this example, the first thing offered up by someone in the group could go in many directions. The seat in our example could have been in an office, on a space shuttle, in a prison cell. The skill is to build the environment one step at a time and not to enter with a pre-conceived idea. If the exercise breaks down or goes off track due to someone blocking or making a suggestion that does not fit, start the exercise again and discuss with the group where and why the exercise went wrong.

Word Up

> Word Up is a team exercise designed to improve vocabulary and speed of thought. It's a team competition that relies on a cool head, steady hand and a good grasp of the English language.

Suitable for

KS3, KS4

Aims

- To extend vocabulary.
- To develop speed of thought.

Resources

- Flipchart and pens/Whiteboard and markers

Space

- Suitable for use in the classroom

What to do

1. Split the group into teams (5 teams of 6 is a good number).
2. Ask the team to line up in rows and give the first person in each row a marker or whiteboard pen. The teams either have to share a whiteboard/flipchart or give the teams one each (you could simply tape a sheet of paper to the wall for each group if easier). Divide the flipchart or whiteboard into 6 sections.
3. The facilitator then calls out a letter of the alphabet and the first person in each row must run to the whiteboard and write as many words as they can, beginning with that letter, in the allocated time. Their team-mates can call out hints, but be warned, this can be very noisy.
4. Once the time limit has elapsed the second member of the team is handed the marker and goes to the board and the teacher calls out a new letter.
5. The team with the most correct words is the winner.

Slide Show

Slide Show is a fantastic exercise to encourage quick thinking and spontaneity. These mock lectures really call for creative responses leading to often hilarious results.

Suitable for

KS3, KS4

Aims

- To develop presentation skills.
- To build on the ideas of others.
- To make creative links.

Resources

- None

Space

- Suitable for use in the classroom

What to do

1. This exercise is for up to 5 players. Assign one member of the group as the 'expert' who is about to give a short presentation on a chosen topic (the topic can be chosen by the group or picked at random from a hat) the other four members of the group are his 'slides'. The 'expert' stands on the left and the 'slides' stand on the right.

2. The expert begins his presentation by facing out to the audience and introducing his first slide. The 4 people (the slides) will instantaneously arrange themselves into an image, striking a pose that the expert must justify by talking us through what it is. Obviously the expert has no idea what they will create or what position they will put

themselves in. Sometimes what they do will compliment his lecture and at other times the lecturer will have to work harder to make the whole thing make sense.

3. The lecture continues until the lecturer says 'In slide 2', at which point the group rearrange themselves into a completely different picture.

4. To begin with try just 3 or 5 slides and get feedback from the group on what works and what doesn't. The best lectures will be when the lecturer can make sense of his slides in the most imaginative and creative way.

Translator

Translator is another great exercise to encourage quick thinking and spontaneity. This time the lecturer can only speak in gibberish. Everything they say is translated into English by their partner. You'll be surprised how informative the whole thing can be.

Suitable for

KS3, KS4

Aims

- To develop listening skills.
- To make creative links.
- To enhance communication skills.

Resources

- None

Space

- Suitable for use in the classroom

What to do

1. This exercise is for 2 people. One person is an expert from a foreign country visiting England to give a lecture on a chosen topic (the topic can be chosen by the group or picked at random from a hat). The guest lecturer can only speak in their native tongue (gibberish) and so the second player must translate everything they say for the audience. The 'expert' stands on the left and the translator stands on the right.

2. The expert begins his presentation by facing out to the audience and talking in gibberish to the audience. The translator must read their body language and listen closely, translating what they hear. The best translations are when what the foreign expert says in gibberish sounds similar to the translation and when the sense of the lecture is being followed.

3. It's always good for the translator to find a suitable ending to the lecture either ending with a few words of wisdom or a quote from the expert lecturer's latest book.

Foreign Film

Foreign Film is an improvised scene calling on the creativity of the actors and the spontaneity of the translators. The actors attempt to recreate the passion of an art house movie, often with ridiculous results.

Suitable for

KS3, KS4

Aims

- To develop listening skills.
- To make creative links.
- To enhance communication skills.

Resources

- None

Space

- Suitable for use in the classroom

What to do

1. This exercise is for 4 people.

2. Two people act out a scene from a foreign language film, speaking only in gibberish. The remaining two players stay on the sidelines, but translate the gibberish into English. After each line of gibberish dialogue is delivered, the actors onstage should give a little pause to allow the two players sitting on the edge time to translate.

3. The two translators should attempt to read the body language of the actors and listen closely, translating exactly what they hear. The best translations are when the gibberish sounds similar to the translation and when the sense of the scene is being followed.

Dubbing

Dubbing is a variation on the Foreign Film exercise. The players attempt to create a seamless voice over to an improvised scene.

Suitable for

KS3, KS4

Aims

- To develop listening skills.
- To make creative links.
- To enhance communication skills.

Resources

- None

Space

- Suitable for use in the classroom

What to do

1. This exercise is for 4 people.

2. Two people act out a scene from a foreign language film. The remaining two players stay on the sidelines, but speak the lines of dialogue which the actors on stage attempt to mouth. The aim is for each actor and their 'voice' to speak in perfect synchronisation, resulting in a perfectly 'dubbed' scene. The actors onstage should attempt to keep the scene physically interesting and the moves they make should influence what is spoken by the 'voices' offstage.

Fictionary

Fictionary is an exercise aimed at developing playful, spontaneous responses. Not only does it require participants to generate new, undiscovered words, it also calls for these words to be justified and defined.

Suitable for

KS3, KS4

Aims

- To develop speed of thought.
- To encourage spontaneity.
- To extend vocabulary.
- To make creative links.

Resources

- None

Space

- Suitable for use in the classroom

What to do

1. This exercise can be played by the whole group.
2. Ask the group to stand in a circle.
3. A volunteer starts by speaking out loud a word that doesn't exist (gibberish).
4. An example might be 'Bardelgook'. The next person in the circle must give that word a definition and describe its meaning.
5. For example 'Bardlegook' is a Norwegian professor who studies the lost works of William Shakespeare.
6. The person who gave the definition must then come up with another gibberish word which is defined and justified by the next person in the group.

Die

Die is a quick-fire word game. Players must tell a story under the guidance of a conductor. The story should flow, with no gaps, hesitations or stumbles. This is a great exercise to encourage listening and to expose the problem of planning too far ahead.

Suitable for

KS3, KS4

Aims

- To develop speed of thought.
- To encourage spontaneity.
- To promote listening and group awareness.

Resources

- None

Space

- Suitable for use in the classroom

What to do

1. Ask 5 people to line up facing the audience. The teacher or facilitator should be the conductor of the story. Ask the audience to choose a character or person from fact or fiction (this could be anyone from William Shakespeare to Godzilla). Also ask the audience to choose a completely unrelated object (e.g. an egg timer).

2. The aim is for the 5 people standing in a line to tell a story that includes both of the suggestions put forward by the audience.

3. The story begins when the conductor points at the first person. Whomever the conductor points at must start speaking and they should continue until the conductor points at someone else in the line. This

person then picks up the story, continuing from the exact moment the previous person finished (even if that was mid-word).

4. The conductor continues to shift the focus at random along the line. There is no order or sequence to the pointing, players must be aware and responsive to the flow of the story, picking it up immediately where the previous player left off.

5. If someone stumbles over a word, makes a mistake or loses their place the audience can shout 'Die'. This person then leaves the stage. This process continues until only one person is left on stage.

Ideally, by this point the line up will have managed to incorporate both of the suggestions given to them by the audience at the start of the game. It is important to give the story a beginning, middle and end. Whoever starts the story should begin by setting the scene, describing where the story takes place and what can be seen, not just jumping straight into the given character and what they are doing. The best stories reveal themselves and the two suggestions (character and object) should be used when required, not right at the start and, ideally, not by the same person.

Chapter 4
Developing Scenes and Stories

Introduction

Writing can sometimes be a challenge, especially in the classroom. Creating scenes and scripts calls for an imaginative approach. How do you structure a monologue? How do you find a starting point for writing a script? How do we excite and encourage students to put pen to paper?

This chapter guides you through a series of exercises designed to help you develop imaginative scenes, stories and monologues and gives a basis for most forms of creative writing. The key to much of the work in this chapter is improvisation. This requires performers to be open and responsive to suggestions, listen attentively to their partners, not to plan ahead (easier said than done) and to trust the exercises to provide the clues as to where to go next.

One Word Story/Conversations

One Word Story is an excellent way to introduce the group to the notion of collaborative storytelling. Through this exercise the group will learn to accept ideas and build on them in order to further the group narrative.

Suitable for

KS3, KS4

Aims

- To promote teamwork.
- To develop speaking and listening skills.
- To understand the principle of 'accept and build'.

Resources

- None

Space

- Classroom or large empty space

What to do

1. Organise the group in a circle and explain that they are going to tell a new story. The only rule is the story must be created one word at a time.

2. The aim is to create a story that is coherent and follows the rules of conventional storytelling. This approach can be used to kick start creative writing exercises.

3. The group could create the introduction to a new tale and then each individual can write the conclusion to the tale, resulting in each person creating a brand new original story from a common starting point. This exercise can also be done in pairs (if the group are finding it difficult).

Variation

- This exercise can also be extended to conversations. Ask individuals in the group to find a partner. Each pair then finds another pair and attempts a conversation (the sentences should be formed one word at a time, speaking in the first person 'I' instead of 'We'). As the pairs get more confident with this skill the facilitator can begin to introduce characters for the pairs to play, still speaking one word at a time.

Alphabet

> Alphabet is a classic exercise that requires performers to listen intently to each other whilst using the structure of the alphabet to inspire the lines of dialogue spoken in the scene.

Suitable for

KS3, KS4

Aims

- To promote speaking and listening.
- To encourage spontaneity.
- To extend use of language.

Resources

- None

Space

- Suitable for use in the classroom

What to do

1. Two volunteers are going to create a scene based on a given topic or location using consecutive letters of the alphabet.
2. First, choose a letter of the alphabet that the conversation will begin with. Then choose a topic or location for the scene to take place.
3. The best way to explain this exercise is to give an example. Let's say the chosen letter is E and the topic is Animals.

   'Enormous Cat you've got Bernard.'

   'Funnily enough he's not even my biggest . . . look at this one.'

   'Good grief he's massive, what have you been feeding him?'

   'Haribo's.'

'Incredible! Is that all he eats?'

'Just Haribo's and Kit Kats.'

'Kit Kats, you can't feed a cat just sweets and chocolate!'

'Look at him, he's not complaining.'

4. The scene continues until the conversation returns to the first letter (E). Each letter of the alphabet must be used including Q and Z. This can sometimes be daunting for students who aren't quick at thinking on their feet, but it's a great brain work out and everyone should be encouraged to at least give it a go.

5. As a development, I've used this technique to encourage creative writing. It provides an excellent, easy to understand structure to writing a group scene, letter or monologue.

Hot Seating

> Hot Seating is a classic drama technique that allows the group to question a character, finding out background information as well as their motives and desires. This exercise also gives participants the chance to experiment with working 'in role'.

Suitable for

KS3, KS4

Aims

- To develop information about character history.
- To encourage students to work 'in role'.
- To create plot and storyline.

Resources

- Character signifiers (items of costume)

Space

- Suitable for use in the classroom

What to do

1. This is an exercise that encourages participants to act 'in role', answering questions about their life, their experiences or about particular events of interest. It gives the group a chance to ask probing questions and build up a character profile.

2. Sit the character on a chair in front of the rest of the group (the Hot Seat) and get the group to ask questions one at a time. If the person in the Hot Seat isn't particularly confident, you could ask the group for questions in advance that could be written on the whiteboard. This allows the person in the Hot Seat more thinking time and will lead to more consistent answers.

3. This exercise calls for a level of spontaneity from the person 'in role'. Remember the aim is to develop the character without giving too much away too quickly. People being interviewed won't necessarily tell everything or tell the whole truth.

4. As more than one person can sit in the Hot Seat and play the same character it may be useful to have items of clothing that signify a particular character like a cap, scarf, coat or bag.

Role on the Wall

Role on the Wall is a visual aid to character development. It can be attached to the wall and added to as more information arises about the character in question.

Suitable for

KS3, KS4

Aims

- To develop information about character history.
- To build a character from scratch.

Resources

- Large sheet of paper (wallpaper/lining paper is ideal)
- Pens or markers

Space

- Suitable for use in the classroom

What to do

1. This is an exercise that allows students to record their thoughts about a character in a visual way. Using a large sheet of paper ask one student to lie on the paper and have someone draw around the outline of this person. You are left with the shape of the character you are currently working on.

2. Inside this shape ask the group to write anything they KNOW about the character (i.e. 10 years old, unhappy, wants to make friends).

3. Outside the figure have the group write anything they FEEL about the character (wants to leave home, is good at poetry).

4. This can then be stuck to the wall or board and returned to from time to time with updates. If we find out one of our hunches is correct then it can be moved inside the figure and becomes fact.

Still Images

> Still Images is one of the fundamental exercises in drama practice. It calls for the group to work together to effectively express a dramatic moment without using movement or words.

Suitable for

KS3, KS4

Aims

- To develop an understanding of key dramatic moments.
- To enhance negotiation skills.
- To effectively convey meaning through physical action .

Resources

- None

Space

- Suitable for use in the classroom

What to do

1. This exercise is best played in groups of 4 or 5.

2. A still image is a frozen moment in time, rather like a photograph. The still image is created physically by the group. The still images can be of a significant moment in time or threaded together to tell a silent story.

3. Try getting the group to tell a famous fairy tale or film using only 5 still images. In order to convey the sense of the whole fairy tale/film they will need to select the key scenes or moments and reproduce these in frozen moments.

4. In order to get the group used to using still images try the 'Appliances' exercise in Chapter 1 (see p. 38).

The Ripple

The Ripple is an excellent way to bring still images to life. The image comes to life one frame at a time allowing the group to build up a sense of meaning slowly and deliberately, building on the previous performers' suggestions.

Suitable for

KS3, KS4

Aims

- To develop an understanding of key dramatic moments.
- To develop speaking and listening skills.
- To understand the principle of 'accept and build'.

Resources

- None

Space

- Suitable for use in the classroom

What to do

1. This exercise is designed to be used exclusively with the Still Images exercise on the previous page.
2. Take a still image that has been created by the group and tell the group that they are going to bring the image to life. They are only allowed to bring the image to life one movement at a time and each person in the still image must move. The group may choose to make one movement and add a line of dialogue, a word or sound to each move, if preferred.
3. The image comes to life in stages in a sort of ripple effect (hence the name The Ripple). The group don't need to bring the image to life immediately, give them the chance to plan and negotiate the best sequence of bringing each character to life.

Sculpting

Sculpting is an instant way to create physical starting points for scenes. The finished sculptures can be interpreted by the group in a variety of ways meaning that each starting point can result in a multitude of different scenes and stories.

Suitable for

KS3, KS4

Aims

- To promote teamwork.
- To develop speaking and listening skills.
- To create instant starting points for scenes.

Resources

- None

Space

- Classroom or large empty space

What to do

1. This exercise can be done in pairs, small groups or as a whole group activity.

Working in pairs

1. Ask people in the group to find a partner and space themselves equidistantly around the room.
2. Ask the pairs to decide on who is A and B in their pairing. A will be the sculptor and B will be the clay. The sculptor (A) cannot speak throughout the sculpting process. This stage of sculpting is really to

allow individuals to experiment with ideas, get used to sculpting someone else and begin to build up confidence and a level of comfort when being physically positioned by another. Shout out an emotion (fear, jubilation, jealousy) and ask A to sculpt B into an image that represents this emotion.

3. If you choose to, once the image has been sculpted, you could allow all the sculptors to walk around the room and look at everyone else's interpretation of the work (although this should also be done without comment or judgement). Once everyone has had a chance to view the work ask all the Bs to relax and swap over so that Bs now sculpt As.

Working in small groups

1. This time arrange people in groups of four, five or six people. Ask the group to select a person to go first (the sculptor). This person now has more clay at their disposal and has more dynamic ways of interpreting a word. Now the words can extend from simple emotions into more challenging themes or topics such as a distant memory, a pointless war, poverty or identity.

2. Give the groups a word and a time limit (say 2 minutes). Again there should be no discussion or planning – the group are positioned exactly as the sculptor intends. Once the time limit is reached you can again let the sculptors take a tour round the other groups to see what has been created.

3. You can also give each group a different theme or topic to work with and have the others in the group try to guess or interpret what has been created. If you choose to try this option make sure that the sculptor or participants of a group don't comment on their own work until the end. What's important is the way an image is perceived by the viewer, even if it's not what was intended by the sculptor. This can lead to good, healthy debate between groups and help the sculptors become more precise when shaping their images.

Working as one whole group

1. Get the group in a circle and ask five volunteers to stand in the centre. This time the clay (or the people in the centre) will sculpt themselves. When a word, emotion or theme is called out the five people in the centre must position themselves in relation to each other in order to capture the essence of the stated word. Again, give the people in the centre a time limit (say 20 seconds) to cut down on thinking time and to make the image spontaneous.

2. Once the people in the centre have settled on their position any of the people standing in the circle can then go in and amend the image by re-sculpting one of the participants. This process can be repeated until the group arrive at an image that everyone agrees sums up the original word. This can take some time, but again the debate is healthy and can lead to some interesting discussions.

3. These exercises can also be used to create the opening image of a scene from where the action can be brought to life. Alternatively, you could select one of the sculpted images as the last scene of a play and ask the group to create five scenes that lead up to that final dramatic moment.

Thought Tracking

> Thought Tracking allows the group to hear key moments in a character's life. Use this technique to discover what someone is thinking at a critical moment in the drama.

Suitable for

KS3, KS4

Aims

- To develop information about a character's history.
- To create the inner monologue of a character.

Resources

- None

Space

- Suitable for use in the classroom

What to do

1. This is an exercise for the whole group.
2. This exercise works particularly well with 'Still Images' (see p. 134). Select a still image that you want to explore further or choose a moment from a scene that the group have created and freeze the action.
3. Ask the rest of the group to approach a frozen character, put their hand on the character's shoulder and say out loud what the character is thinking at that precise moment.
4. This works best if the person speaking the thoughts uses the first person, for example 'I wish I had more friends,' rather than 'He's thinking about having more friends.'
5. Every member of the group can approach a character and deliver an internal thought. This is a great exercise to uncover hidden truths about a character, contributing to a deeper character analysis.

Conscience Alley

Conscience Alley is a way for the group to advise a character before they make an important decision in the drama. It gives participants the chance to consider alternatives and state the case for what they would do in the character's position.

Suitable for

KS3, KS4

Aims

- To develop information about character history.
- To give advice to a character.
- To consider alternatives.

Resources

- None

Space

- Suitable for use in the classroom

What to do

1. This is an exercise for the whole group.
2. This exercise works particularly well just before a character makes a life-changing decision. Ask the group to line up in two lines, shoulder to shoulder, facing each other so that they form a corridor.
3. Ask the character to stand at one end of the corridor. As they walk down the corridor (this should be done slowly) the people in the lines can either give words of advice (positive and negative) or speak the inner thoughts of the character.

4. If we take an example of a young girl preparing to run away from home, the girl will stand at the end of the corridor, bags packed, and walk slowly down the path. She might hear,

'Your mum and dad will be devastated when they find out,' or 'Run as fast as you can you know you're doing the right thing.'

Alternatively the group may say the characters internal thoughts (as in Thought Tracking).

The character may hear,

'I hope I'm making the right decision,' or 'I bet they don't even notice I'm gone.'

Diary Entry

> Diary Entry is an excellent way to get into the mind of a character and create background information about their relationships, thought processes and emotional state.

Suitable for

KS3, KS4

Aims

- To develop information about character history.
- To create plot and storyline.
- To enhance creative writing.

Resources

- Paper
- Pens

Space

- Suitable for use in the classroom

What to do

1. This is a writing exercise.
2. Select a character from a famous work of fiction or use a character that the group have created. Place the character at an important point in their development or at a time when they have a significant decision to make.
3. Ask the group to write a diary entry for the character. This can be done as a whole group, one line at a time, or individually. The diary entry will give an insight into the mindset of the character and their emotional state.
4. The diary entry can be started in any way suitable for the character in question. If writing for fictional characters that the group have created try starting with 'Dear Diary'.

Words of Wisdom

Words of Wisdom relies on spontaneity and the ability not to block your initial thoughts and ideas. Similar to One Word Story (see p. 127) this exercise will have the group speaking like a great sage in no time.

Suitable for

KS3, KS4

Aims

- To develop speed of thought.
- To enhance vocabulary.
- To develop speaking and listening skills.
- To understand the principle of 'accept and build'.

Resources

- None

Space

- Suitable for use in the classroom

What to do

1. This exercise is similar to 'One Word Story/Conversation'.
2. Stand the group in a circle and ask one volunteer to start a proverb or inspirational saying. As this exercise is played one word at a time there is no scope for planning. The words of wisdom generated will at times make sense and be insightful; at other times they will be ridiculous and meaningless. Either way, the games should be played with reverie and the intensity of a sage or great thinker.
3. The words of wisdom can be short or long, it is up to the group to find a suitable end to the sentence. It's difficult for me to give an example playing it by myself, but here are some possible, nonsensical sayings:

A – Light, **B** – Is, **C** – There, **D** – Then, **A** – It's, **B** – Not.
A – Take, **B** – Your, **C** – Time, **D** – To, **A** – See, **B** – Yourself.
A – Pain, **B** – Hurts.

4. This exercise can then be used to create scenes or monologues. Write down the most memorable words of wisdom created by the group. Ask them either to create a scene in which as many of the words of wisdom are spoken or individually to write a monologue that includes three of their favourites.

5. If they choose to create a scene using the words of wisdom, ask them first to consider what type of character would be most likely to utter those words – would it be a mother, shopkeeper, doctor? Then ask them to choose a location for the scene to take place and decide who else would be there in the scene.

6. The skill lies in creating a believable piece of drama, where the words of wisdom blend seamlessly into the scene or monologue.

Cross Fade

Cross Fade is a film technique adapted here to work for the stage. The aim is to heighten the meaning of a given text by contrasting it with another to bring out potential hidden links.

Suitable for

KS3, KS4

Aims

- To analyse two contrasting texts or scenes.
- To develop a sense of theatrical staging.
- To create new meaning from prescribed text.

Resources

- Scenes from existing dramatic works

Space

- Empty space

What to do

1. Essentially a film technique which allows the group to cross fade between two scenes.
2. Ask pupils to devise or rehearse two scenes that happen in different locations or at different times (they could be from totally different plays). Ask them to find ways of editing the scenes so that there is a seamless cross fade between the two.
3. This can be done with an existing script (e.g. *Romeo and Juliet*) or student-devised scene based on a particular theme. The aim is to find the best points to cut between the scenes, maybe echoing lines or meaning in the scene and highlighting similarities in the way the scene is staged.
4. Try to present the scenes on opposite sides of the stage and alternate between the two.

Character Bridge

Character Bridge asks the group to explore ways in which two characters can be brought closer together. Students fill the gap by suggesting the ways their differences can be resolved.

Suitable for

KS3, KS4

Aims

- To understand alternate viewpoints.
- To heighten understanding of a character.

Resources

- None

Space

- Suitable for use in the classroom

What to do

1. This is basically a technique for understanding more about what can bring two people closer.
2. Choose two characters from a book, play or even a television show. Stand two people at opposite ends of the room and get them to declare their feelings for each other or the situation they find themselves in.
3. Then one by one ask the other members of the group to fill the space between them. As each new person adds a section of the 'Bridge' they should say out loud something that will bring the two characters closer together or something that will resolve their differences.
4. Keep adding to the 'Bridge' until the two characters have been joined together.

N.S.E.W.

N.S.E.W. allows the group to create instant, whole group images around epic themes. This exercise provides a great starting point for creative writing or scene work.

Suitable for

KS3, KS4

Aims

- To encourage fluidity of movement.
- To enhance group awareness.
- To develop a sense of theatrical staging.
- To create instant starting points for scenes.

Resources

- None

Space

- Empty space

What to do

1. Arrange the group in a group or clump in the centre of the space. Each person must be making physical contact with at least two other people. This should be as subtle as possible i.e. back to back or simply brushing shoulders or making contact with feet next to each other. Everyone will be in contact with someone in a different way, nothing is uniform.

2. Point out for the group the points of a compass in relation to where they are standing, North, South, East and West. Ask the group to turn, over a slow count of ten, to face a new direction. The group must remain in contact with two people at all times as they turn. Ask them to experiment with levels so that not everyone in the group is simply standing.

3. Once the group has mastered turning to face a specified compass point you can then add in an emotion that they can display when they reach their final co-ordinate. For example you could say 'I want you to face South over the count of ten with jubilation,' before beginning your slow count to ten. The group then slowly turn staying in contact with two other people in the group at all times and slowly grow into an image of jubilation.

4. This is an instant image, created by the group without verbal communication. You can even ask members of the group to step out of the final image to see what they have created.

Group Monologue

Group Monologue takes the pressure off writing as an individual. In this exercise everyone works together to create a speech one line at a time.

Suitable for

KS3, KS4

Aims

- To develop speaking and listening skills.
- To understand the principle of 'accept and build'.
- To promote teamwork.

Resources

- Pens and card or
- A flip chart

Space

- Suitable for use in a classroom

What to do

1. Tell the class that they are about to write a monologue (it could be a random monologue or based on a character from a book). They will write it as a group one line at a time.
2. Ask for a volunteer to start the process by supplying one line.
3. Tell the group not to worry about how it sounds because there will be a chance to edit and rearrange the lines at the end.

Variation

- An alternative to this exercise is to give everyone 5 cards each and ask them to write 5 different lines on them. Then bring the group together and select one card to start the monologue. Ask people to add to the monologue by offering any card that seems to lead on or make sense of the previous line. (This is a random process but you'll be surprised at how things develop and how much sense the finished product actually makes.)

Photo Fit

Photo Fit is a creative way to bring a character to life. This technique builds a character through a blend of insightful questioning and imaginative assumptions.

Suitable for

KS3, KS4

Aims

- To build up a realistic character profile.
- To develop questioning skills.
- To enhance creative writing.

Resources

- Photographs
- Pens
- Paper
- Envelopes

Space

- Suitable for use in the classroom

What to do

1. Select a photograph from a magazine or newspaper of somebody who is not famous (it may be best to use local papers rather than tabloids or broadsheets).
2. Cut out the photo and write a series of questions that will help you build up a more detailed understanding of this person.

3. Put the photo and your list of questions in an envelope and give it to someone else in the room. It is their job to answer the questions and then return the envelope to you. Once you have received the envelope and answers back, write a short monologue that the person in the picture might say.

4. This exercise is about asking the right questions. If the questions are answered imaginatively then the final monologue may highlight some strong characteristics.

5. Once everyone in the room has written a monologue take the exercise a step further by joining forces with another person in the room and writing a duologue using your new characters. How would these two people interact? Where would they be likely to meet?

Soundscape

Soundscape is an excellent way to create atmosphere for a scene. This exercise also allows you to create narrative without concentrating on what is happening but, rather, focusing on what can be heard.

Suitable for

KS3, KS4

Aims

- To develop speaking and listening skills.
- To enhance story and plot development.
- To develop information about character history.
- To generate information about character relationships.

Resources

- None

Space

- Suitable for use in a classroom

What to do

- Split the class into groups of 5 or 6. The aim is to create the sounds of an event, incident or scene without using movement or physical performance. The event could be a moment from a character's life (first day at school) or a more abstract dream or nightmare.

Variations

- Alternatively, you could give each group an image of a specific place and ask them to create the noises that can be heard in that location (old derelict house, busy street, doctor's waiting room). Ideally, the Soundscape should involve spoken words as well as just sounds. This gives an opportunity to discover a character's inner voice or find out more about other people's thoughts and opinions of a character.
- This exercise works well in conjunction with the Dreamscape exercise on the following page.

Dreamscape

Dreamscape is a way of displaying the inner turmoil of a character, physically. The dreams are created in complete silence placing the focus on what happens, rather than what can be heard.

Suitable for

KS3, KS4

Aims

- To develop physical and group awareness.
- To enhance story and plot development.
- To develop information about character history.
- To generate information about character relationships.

Resources

- None

Space

- Suitable for use in a classroom

What to do

1. Follow the same set up as the Soundscape exercise and break the class into groups of 5 or 6.

2. The aim this time is to create just the images of a dream or nightmare through physical movement. The dream could be about somebody's first day at school.

3. Try choosing one group to create the dreamscape and another group to create the Soundscape. Ideally the Soundscape should involve

spoken words as well as just sounds. This provides an opportunity to discover a character's inner voice or find out more about other people's thoughts and opinions of a character.

4. Have the two groups work separately and then bring the two parts together playing them at the same time. It may be a little disjointed, but that's how dreams and nightmares appear to us anyway.

Ten-word Cascade

Ten-word Cascade is an excellent structure to enhance creative writing. This exercise allows the scene to build gradually and controls the number of words used.

Suitable for

KS3, KS4

Aims

- To enhance the use of vocabulary.
- To generate imaginative responses.
- To create effective material working within a given structure.

Resources

- None

Space

- Suitable for use in a classroom

What to do

1. This is a simple, easy to follow structure for people new to creating scripted or improvised scenes. The first line in the scene can only contain one word; the second line contains two, the third line three words and so on up to ten words in the last line of the scene.

   For example,

   A – Morning.

   B – Morning Jim.

   A – Where's Harry today?

   B – He's not feeling well.

   A – He was off last week.

   B – I don't really think he's ill.

> A – I heard he's got a new job.
> B – Really, don't you think we should tell somebody?
> A – Why? It's none of our business what Harry does.
> B – We're the ones having to do twice as much work.
>
> **2.** This is a great writing exercise, as the structure really dictates the flow of the scene. It also encourages writers to think about use of language and editing their work appropriately. If necessary, once the scene has reached the designated ten-word limit you can also work back down from ten to one, ending the scene with a single word.

Variation

- There are many variations of this exercise which may be of use depending on age and ability of group. First, you could invert the game and start with ten words in the first line working your way down through the numbers till you reach one. Alternatively, to make it shorter and slightly easier, start with five words, working your way through one and back to five.

Hidden Thoughts

Hidden Thoughts allows us to hear what a character really thinks, giving us a unique insight into how they feel about the people around them.

Suitable for

KS3, KS4

Aims

- To develop information about character history.
- To generate information about character relationships.

Resources

- None

Space

- Suitable for use in the classroom

What to do

1. This is an exercise for four players.
2. Two players are on stage improvising a scene and the other two players sit on the edge of the stage. After each line of dialogue is delivered the actors onstage should give a little pause to allow the two players sitting on the edge to say what the characters onstage really think.
3. As this calls for the players to improvise, it may be easier and less threatening to set the location and indicate who each person is before the scene starts (for a list of scene starters see pp. 206–209).

Example

Actor 1	I've finished the report sir.
Hidden Thought 1	*I hope I get this promotion.*
Actor 2	That looks good Simon, thanks for that.
Hidden Thought 2	*About time too, I asked for it last week.*
Actor 1	I've put in for more overtime sir, I know we need to win this contract.
Hidden Thought 1	*I really should be spending more time at home.*
Actor 2	We need people like you Simon; times are tough at the moment.
Hidden Thought 2	*Creep!*

Park Bench

In this game, one person decides the character for both participants. The other participant has to react to this while trying to determine their character.

Suitable for

KS3, KS4

Aims

- To develop sensitivity and awareness.
- To encourage speaking and listening.
- To build on the ideas of others.
- To create story and plot.

Resources

- Chairs

Space

- Suitable for use in the classroom

What to do

1. Place three chairs onstage or in the performance area, this is your park bench. Ask one volunteer to sit on the bench.
2. The setting is a park, and the person on the bench has no character until the second performer enters. The second performer should decide both who they are and who the person sitting on the park bench is.

3. For example, the person entering could decide that the person on the bench is their father, who has just stormed out after a huge row at home and they have come to find him. Alternatively the person on the bench could be a famous actor and they are their biggest fan.

4. The performer sitting on the bench must adapt to whatever situation is presented to them, listening attentively and developing their character bit by bit. The improvisation ends when one actor finds a reason to exit and the audience are asked to identify who the two characters were.

A Scene with no 'S'

A great exercise to re-engage performers with what they are saying, asking them to think before speaking, contributing to a more thoughtful, rounded scene.

Suitable for

KS3, KS4

Aims

- To extend vocabulary.
- To develop speaking and listening.
- To create effective material working within a given structure.

Resources

- None

Space

- Suitable for use in the classroom

What to do

1. The performers in this exercise must avoid using words containing the letter 'S' in their scene. If somebody makes a mistake, as no doubt they will, replace that performer with someone else and have the scene continue from the point the mistake was made.

2. This is an excellent exercise that not only engages the performers on stage but also the audience as they need to remain alert and listen out for any words containing the dreaded letter 'S'. It may take some practice to master in performance, but this exercise can also make a great structure for written scenes and stories.

Variation

- Play a scene restricting the use of other letters. Try not to banish any vowels and don't place more than one restricted letter on a scene at any one time.

What's a Question?

What's a Question? is a similar exercise to 'A Scene with no 'S''. It allows performers to build a scene with full focus on what they say.

Suitable for

KS3, KS4

Aims

- To extend vocabulary.
- To develop speaking and listening.
- To enhance self-awareness.
- To create effective material working within a given structure.

Resources

- None

Space

- Suitable for use in the classroom

What to do

1. The performers in this exercise must avoid using questions in the scene they are creating. If somebody makes a mistake, as no doubt they will, replace that performer with someone else and have the scene continue from the point the mistake was made.

2. This is more difficult than it first appears. We normally use questions to elicit information from our fellow performers, especially in improvised scenes. This encourages actors to make positive statements and bold choices in the creation of the scene. Ask the audience to stay alert, listen out for any questions and be ready to replace performers when mistakes are made. This exercise also makes a great structure for written scenes and stories.

Every Other Question

This is a similar exercise to 'What's a Question?' This, however, encourages the use of questions to propel the development of the scene.

Suitable for

KS3, KS4

Aims

- To extend vocabulary.
- To develop speaking and listening.
- To enhance self-awareness.
- To create effective material working within a given structure.

Resources

- None

Space

- Suitable for use in the classroom

What to do

1. One performer in this exercise is encouraged to end every sentence they speak with a question (hence every other line being a question). The other performer responds as normal with no restriction on the lines they deliver, this performer also starts the scene. For example,

   A – Hey Jerry I've got a message for you from the boss.
   B – What does he want now?
   A – He says he's not happy with productivity and he wants the whole department to stay late.
   B – What?
   A – Hey don't shoot the messenger!

B – Is he having a laugh?

A – Look Jerry, I've heard they're looking to make people redundant, don't go rocking the boat.

B – I've got a young family waiting for me at home, did you tell him that?

A – It's not my place mate, he's in his office if you want a word.

B – It's not your place? You're supposed to be his right hand man aren't you?

A – Look I'm not getting involved, I've given you my advice, you can take it or leave it.

2. This structure doesn't power a scene along, but it gives the actor something to focus on and can help students when writing short bursts of dialogue.

Variation

- This time try every other line spoken by each character being limited to a question or every third line spoken in the scene must be a question. As a writing exercise this can help to structure the work and also drive the scene along quicker than in the previous version.

Last Letter Scenes

> A great exercise to encourage performers to listen to each other, to take their time before responding and build upon offers made.

Suitable for

KS3, KS4

Aims

- To develop speed of thought.
- To heighten concentration.
- To enhance vocabulary.
- To improve speaking and listening.

Resources

- None

Space

- Suitable for use in the classroom

What to do

1. This exercise builds on 'Last Letter' (see p. 110). Performers are asked to create a scene where each line uses the last letter of the previous line as the start of the sentence. For example,

   A – Drag the body over here.

   B – Everybody said you were a nasty piece of work.

   A – Keep dragging, this isn't the time or place for an argument.

   B – This is wrong; we're going to get caught.

   A – Tom listen, you're part of this now, you can't just walk away.

   B – You think I'm afraid of you?

2. This exercise frees the performer from worrying about what comes next and requires them to listen to the previous sentence before deciding on a response. This structure can also be used as a creative writing exercise in the classroom.

The Creative Touch

This exercise generates scenes without relying heavily on language. Use physical contact between characters to build and enhance your scene making skills.

Suitable for

KS3, KS4

Aims

- To make creative links.
- To justify actions.
- To encourage physical contact.

Resources

- None

Space

- Suitable for use in the classroom

What to do

1. In order to speak, the performers in this exercise must touch each other making physical contact that is relevant to the scene (shaking hands, pushing their fellow actor, holding hands, touching their partner on the shoulder). Any form of contact is acceptable as long as it is realistic and appropriate for the development of the scene.
2. The aim is to find clever ways of linking physical contact with the words being spoken. Build the scene slowly and attempt to justify the reason behind each moment of contact.

Freeze Tag

 This is primarily an exercise for developing spontaneity, but also a great exercise for creating quick-fire scenes.

Suitable for

KS3, KS4

Aims

- To develop speed of thought.
- To heighten concentration.
- To encourage physical contact.
- To justify actions.

Resources

- None

Space

- Suitable for use in the classroom

What to do

1. Ask two performers to enter the performance space. Give them both a physical position to start in (e.g. one may be crouching down; the other may be looking through binoculars). Ask the actors to play a scene inspired by this starting point.
2. When the audience see the actors in another interesting position someone can shout 'Freeze'. Both actors freeze exactly where they are and the audience member who froze the action enters the scene and tags one of the actors out, replacing them by taking up their exact physical position.
3. The two actors now start a completely new scene using their positions as the new starting point.

Typewriter

Typewriter is a story building exercise that uses performers to illustrate and bring the story to life. A narrative based exercise that stretches the creativity of narrator and performers alike.

Suitable for

KS3, KS4

Aims

- To develop speed of thought.
- To generate imaginative ideas.
- To enhance vocabulary.

Resources

- None

Space

- Suitable for use in the classroom

What to do

1. One volunteer sits in a chair positioned to one side of the performance space. A group of up to eight performers sit on the other side of the stage leaving the centre of the stage empty.

2. The writer mimes typing on a typewriter and narrates the story they are creating. As the writer describes the scene the performance group move centre stage and begin to act out the story, creating characters, producing sound effects and even becoming part of the set if required.

Sixty-second Trailer

This is a great exercise in negotiation, determining what makes a film/story work and what important elements must be retained to give the film its identity.

Suitable for

KS3, KS4

Aims

- To enhance negotiation skills.
- To recognise key dramatic moments.
- To develop a sense of team.

Resources

- None

Space

- Suitable for use in the classroom

What to do

1. The aim of this exercise is to take a well known film or book and condense it into a trailer of sixty seconds. The only restriction is the events shown must all be in chronological order, giving the trailer a beginning, middle and end.

2. Give the group time to work on this and negotiate which elements of the story are important, which lines are necessary to identify the film and who is to play which characters.

3. Let the other members of the class guess which film it is.

Variation

- Ask one person to attempt this, outlining the plot, playing all the characters and presenting all the necessary information.

Rooms

This is a great improvisation exercise. One person switches between two scenes but they have no idea what scene they will be taking part in until they walk into the room.

Suitable for

KS3, KS4

Aims

- To develop spontaneity.
- To enhance creative thinking.
- To improve speaking and listening.

Resources

- None

Space

- Suitable for use in the classroom

What to do

1. Set up the space so that you have two spaces, one stage left and one stage right (see website for a diagram of stage areas).

2. Have two actors stand stage left and two actors stage right. These are rooms, rooms where scenes will take place (these rooms can be marked out in chalk or tape if required). The space in between the room acts as a corridor.

3. Ask a volunteer (C) to enter one of the rooms. Immediately upon entering the scene begins, led by the two actors (A and B) who are already in the room. A and B give C all the information they need to work out who they are and where they are. For example,

C enters the room.

A – Well, well, well if it isn't Darren Guest. Take a seat son, what is it this time GBH, shoplifting?

B – Thought you were going straight Darren, what's the matter? Couldn't hack it?

A – Right Darren, got anything to say off the record before we start the interview?

C – I'm not telling you two anything. What you gonna do put me back inside? I'll be out in a month or two.

4. C only begins to add to the scene once they've got a clear indication from the other two actors of where they are and who they are. This is a great exercise to develop support between performers and building spontaneous thinking and improvisation skills.

5. Once the scene has been established and we know who all the people in the scene are and where it's taking place, A or B find a reason to leave the room. Once they've left they stop playing their character and return to neutral before walking into the next room (they enter this room as a C). As soon as they enter room two, exactly the same process is followed and they take their lead from A and B. Meanwhile in the room they have left both players are replaced by new actors and they wait for the next person to enter their room.

6. It's important that no planning takes place before C enters a room. This exercise is not necessarily about creating fantastic scenes, it's about discovering how to support your fellow performers and what information is required so the audience can establish where a scene is taking place and the relationship between the people in it.

7. After a few scenes it's always good to discuss the merits of each and unpick what worked and how performers managed to reveal the location of their scene.

Emotional Grid

This is a great exercise to aid the development of scene work. The layout of the stage gives structure and content to the scene and takes the actors mind off the pressure of developing a storyline.

Suitable for

KS3, KS4

Aims

- To develop spontaneity.
- To improve speaking and listening.
- To enhance spatial awareness.
- To create effective material working within a given structure.
- To justify character actions.

Resources

- None

Space

- Suitable for use in the classroom

What to do

1. When first attempting this exercise it's best to work with just two participants.
2. Divide the stage into six sections, these sections can be visualised by the actors or marked out physically with tape or chalk. Each of the six sections onstage is assigned an emotion or state of being (fear, kindness, suspicion, anger, indecision, desire). The actors act out a scene and must match their emotions during the course of the scene to the area in which they are standing.

Desire	Indecision
Anger	Suspicion
Kindness	Fear

3. Imagine actor A starts in the kindness section of the stage and the other actor B starts in the suspicion section. It's a scene between a couple who have just split up and have arranged to meet for one last time.

A – Hi Martin, thanks for coming.

B – That's all right. What do you want?

A – Nothing, I just thought we could chat.

B – About what? What have you got planned Sarah?

A – Relax. Here have one of these.

B – What is it?

A – What does it look like, it's a cake.

B – What's in it?

A – Erm, just the usual, flour, eggs, a bit of sugar. You used to like a cake or two. I made them especially for you.

B – Yeah I bet you did. Just because we can't be together, you want rid of me don't you? They're probably spiked.

(A walks into the anger section of the stage.)

A – Look why do you always treat me like this? I'm sick of it. I try to do something nice for you and you throw it back in my face. You've hurt me, you know, and now you're going to pay for it.

(B walks into the fear section of the stage.)

B – What do you mean? What are you going to do?

(A pulls out a gun.)

B – What the hell are you doing? Please don't. Sarah you're making a big mistake. Please! Think about all the good times.

A – You're going to find out what it's like to be me. Kneel down and close your eyes.

B – (Doing what she says.) Sarah please, you've got this all wrong. I never meant to hurt you.

(A moves into the indecision section of the stage, she looks confused, she's finding it hard to go through with it.)

4. As this example shows, emotions aren't always shown verbally. Encourage students to take their time and let the scene build naturally. Actors can remain in one section for a long time or, if necessary, move quickly between the sections. The grid is designed to help the actor build a realistic scene and push the storyline along. Don't use this exercise as a gimmick by rushing between sections and creating a scene with no coherence.

Variations

- Once the group have the hang of this exercise try only allowing one actor to be activated by the emotions in the grid. Let the other actor(s) just respond naturally and see if this enhances or detracts from the scene work. If the group get particularly confident with this exercise try splitting the stage into nine sections instead of six.

- You could also use this as a writing exercise as I've done in the example above. Give each person a grid with pre-selected emotions on and ask them to write a script that can be performed by other members of the group.

- An excellent variation is to assign each section a number (1 to 6) instead of an emotion. Write or choose a script that involves 6 performers and have the group act out the scene whilst adhering to the numbers in each square. If an actor stands in square two another actor must join him and the rest must position themselves in square four. If someone moves into square six all the other actors must find a reason to justify joining him in that square.

Sit, Stand, Lie

This is an improvisation exercise for three players. The scene is dictated by the position of each actor on stage which takes the actors' mind off developing text and story, allowing the scene to build organically.

Suitable for

KS3, KS4

Aims

- To develop spontaneity.
- To improve speaking and listening.
- To enhance spatial awareness.
- To create effective material working within a given structure.
- To justify character actions.

Resources

- None

Space

- Suitable for use in the classroom

What to do

1. Three actors perform an improvised scene. Ask the audience to suggest a location for the scene.

2. One actor must always be sitting; one actor standing and the final actor must be lying down. If one actor changes position i.e. from lying down to standing, the other actors must adapt their positions accordingly.

3. Each time an actor changes position the actor must justify the move; there must be a reason for the repositioning.

4. Whilst this exercise is fun, the aim is to attempt to build a coherent scene that is supported by the positioning restriction rather than being hindered by it.

Variation

- If lying down is proving too difficult (it can be tricky to justify) try having one actor crouch or kneel.

First Line, Last Line

This is an improvisation exercise for two players. The performers must develop the scene only knowing what the first and last lines will be.

Suitable for

KS3, KS4

Aims

- To develop spontaneity.
- To improve speaking and listening.
- To develop story and plot.
- To create effective material working within a given structure.

Resources

- None

Space

- Suitable for use in the classroom

What to do

1. Two actors perform an improvised scene. The only lines pre-decided in the scene are the first and last lines. You can ask the audience to suggest lines or the teacher can choose lines that are suitable from the back of this book.

2. The aim is to perform a coherent scene linking the first and last lines. Outside the first and last line the scene is completely improvised. If you need inspiration, please see the appendices for suggestions of suitable first and last lines of dialogue (see p. 207).

Variation

- Normally both actors know what the first and last line of the scene is. This way they can both work towards a resolution together. However, you could try giving one actor the first line and the other actor the last line. This puts more pressure on the actor with the final line as they must listen intently, looking for an opportunity to end the scene.

Fish Bowl

This is a great exercise that requires performers to justify lines of dialogue that are selected at random throughout the scene.

Suitable for

KS3, KS4

Aims

- To develop spontaneity.
- To improve speaking and listening.
- To develop story and plot.
- To create effective material working within a given structure.
- To justify character actions.

Resources

- None

Space

- Suitable for use in the classroom

What to do

1. This is an exercise for two or three performers.

2. Everyone in the group is asked to write a line of dialogue on a slip of paper. This piece of paper is then folded and placed into a hat, container or, as the name implies, fish bowl. The container is placed on the stage so that it is easily accessible by each performer.

3. The performers are then asked to improvise a scene, the location or relationship between the characters can be decided by the group or the teacher. The actors play the scene and at random points throughout they choose a line of dialogue from the container, open it

and read it. The line of dialogue must be woven into the sense of the scene, being justified by either the person who read out the line or another actor onstage.

4. It is usually wise to set the scene up first, establishing the Who? What? Where? before picking lines of dialogue to incorporate into the scene.

Puppets

Puppets is about accepting offers and responding to the demands made by the puppet masters. The aim is to play a scene that fully justifies the positions that the performers find themselves in.

Suitable for

KS3, KS4

Aims

- To encourage spontaneity.
- To work effectively with a partner.
- To improve speaking and listening.
- To enhance spatial awareness.
- To justify character actions.

Resources

- None

Space

- Suitable for use in the classroom

What to do

1. This exercise is best played with 4 people. Two people are performers (puppets) and the other two are puppet masters.

2. The puppet masters move the puppets around the stage, physically moulding and shaping their movements and expressions. The puppets must perform a scene, influenced by the positions they are placed in by their puppet masters.

3. If, for example, a performer's hand is placed on their stomach by their puppet master the performer must justify this move by saying, 'Oh I'm not feeling too well, I've had an upset stomach for the last few days.'

4. The other puppet master may make their performer wave and this must be built into the scene, e.g. 'There's Melissa; she'll know what to do she's a nurse.'

5. The puppet masters can move their puppets around the stage and the best way to get someone to walk is to tap them gently behind the knee. It can sometimes be difficult to lift your puppet partner's leg and expect them to keep their balance.

6. This exercise calls for quick thinking and the ability to play along with the puppet master. It's an enjoyable game that can often result in hilarious scenes. Played well, it can produce some surprising results and relies heavily on good teamwork and understanding.

Who? What? Where?

Who, What, Where are the fundamental building blocks on which good scene work thrives. Practise this exercise on a regular basis, the more proficient the group get at this the better their resulting scene work will be.

Suitable for

KS3, KS4

Aims

- To develop spontaneity.
- To improve speaking and listening.
- To justify character actions.

Resources

- None

Space

- Suitable for use in the classroom

What to do

1. This exercise can be played by two, three or four players.
2. Essentially the structure to this exercise is loose. It relies heavily on improvisation. Nothing is planned before the performers take to the stage.
3. Ask one performer to enter the space first. They establish the scene by miming an activity that gives the actor offstage an idea of either who they are, where they are or what they are doing.

Example

The first actor mimes blowing up a balloon, this may suggest that they are preparing for a party. The second actor could then enter and say, 'This place looks great darling; our Stacey is going to love this party. I can't believe she's six already.'

The first actor might reply 'Come on, give us a hand John, we're behind schedule, people will be arriving soon. (She looks around.) Are you sure a Working Men's Club is suitable for a six year old's birthday?'

The second actor says, 'Oh stop panicking, it was cheap. Besides it was all I could get.'

4. The idea is that the audience should be able to work out, in the shortest time possible, who the characters are (husband and wife), where they are (in a Working Men's Club) and what they are doing (setting up for their daughter's birthday party).

The Walls Have Ears

This is an exercise that creates back story by using a specific location. The idea is that walls soak up our words, rather like sponges. Over the years the walls have heard many conversations and the lines and words spoken remain embedded in the walls themselves.

Suitable for

KS3, KS4

Aims

- To generate imaginative responses.
- To enhance creative writing.
- To develop a character profile.

Resources

- None

Space

- Suitable for use in the classroom

What to do

1. This exercise is suitable for the whole group.

2. Ask the group to create the four walls of a room by standing in lines, shoulder to shoulder and facing into the room they are creating. The room should have a relevance to a particular character or play an important role in the story (e.g. a prison cell, kitchen where an important incident took place, an interview room).

3. The group speak one at a time creating lines that may have been 'soaked up' by the walls over the years. This exercise is usually done

with no pre-planning or preparation. If necessary though, you can always give the group time to consider their lines.

4. These words, lines or sounds that have been created by the group can now be incorporated into a scene or script. If people create intriguing lines ask the group when the line was spoken, who was in the room at the time, where the characters were standing.

5. This exercise leads seamlessly into creative writing and is an immediate way of pinpointing key moments in a story without worrying about the pressure of creating the whole scene.

New Choice

New Choice is an exercise that calls for quick responses and spontaneity. Performers are guided by another team member offstage who prompts more interesting alternatives to what has already been said.

Suitable for

KS3, KS4

Aims

- To develop spontaneity.
- To improve speaking and listening.
- To develop story and plot.
- To encourage more imaginative responses.

Resources

- None

Space

- Suitable for use in the classroom

What to do

1. This exercise is best performed in threes.
2. Two people are the performers who improvise a standard scene. Every so often, the third player (who is off stage) will say 'New choice'. At this point the last line spoken must be replaced with something new. The aim is for the person off stage to guide and direct the performers onstage to make choices that benefit the construction of the scene.
3. This example is based on two young work colleagues getting ready for their Christmas night out:

A – So Phil, are you ready for the big night?

B – Yep, I've never been readier! I can't wait for tonight.

A – I heard Sandra's going to be there.

B – Who's Sandra?

New choice

B – Sandra from accounts?

New choice

B – Sandra's my sister Dave; you better not try any funny business.

A – All right relax; I'm just saying she's going to be there. Anyway she's not my type she's too small.

New choice

A – She's too tall.

New choice

A – She's too giggly.

New choice

A – She's too wide.

B – Wide, wide, are you saying my sister is fat?

A – No.

New choice

A – Yes.

B – Well thanks Dave, thanks for that. I happen to know she's got a soft spot for you.

4. This is an excellent exercise that forces first-time improvisers to keep generating more and more ideas. It also gives the performers (and the audience) an insight into what works in a scene and what doesn't.

Prompts

In this exercise an offstage 'prompt' helps to guide the action and drive forward the scene. Excellent exercise for new improvisers and for those who always claim they don't know what to say.

Suitable for

KS3, KS4

Aims

- To develop spontaneity.
- To improve speaking and listening.
- To enhance teamwork and support.
- To encourage more imaginative responses.

Resources

- None

Space

- Suitable for use in the classroom

What to do

1. This exercise is best played by 3 or 4 people.

2. Ask two performers to improvise a scene. The scene can be about anything (you can use locations or starting lines at the back of this book if you need inspiration).

3. Have one of the performers in role as someone who is terrible at learning lines (even though the scene is fully improvised). Ask this performer to shout 'Prompt' whenever they need help in remembering the end of their line.

   Another person is 'offstage' and acts as the prompt, quickly supplying lines when called upon. The prompt can fill in one word for the performer onstage or provide them with a whole line. For example, imagine a scene between boyfriend and girlfriend at a train station.

Boy – Well I suppose this is it.
Girl – Don't worry, I'll be back every weekend. I won't forget you.
Boy – I hope not. Before you go I've got something for you.
Girl – A present, oh Darren you shouldn't have.
Boy – It's nothing really, it's a, a . . . *'prompt'*
Prompt – Book about sea fishing
Girl – Fishing?
Boy – Yeah well, I thought as you're going to Uni in Brighton, with very little money. It might just come in handy; you could catch your own food.
Girl – Great, thanks. Look Darren the train's about to leave.
Boy – Well, bye then. Will you, erm . . .*'prompt'*. . .
Prompt – Call me everyday.
Girl – Of course I will.
Boy – And . . .*'prompt'* . . .
Prompt – Tell me if you've caught anything.
Girl – Caught anything?
Boy – Yeah, fish. Let me know if the book pays off.
Girl – Oh Darren, I'm going to miss you. Come here give me a kiss.
(They kiss and wave goodbye.)

4. As shown in this example, it's probably best to have a few lines to establish the scene before asking for 'prompts'. It's also important for the performer who asks for the 'prompt' to justify whatever line is fed to them.

5. As you can imagine this scene could simply descend into nonsense and stupidity very easily. The real skill is for the 'prompt' to help to build a relevant and sensible scene whilst throwing in a few strange lines that the actors must work hard to justify.

Variation

- Have a prompt for both performers on stage, or allow both performers to ask for prompts from the same person. This can get messy and confusing so only experiment with it once the group are comfortable with the original version.

Silent Scenes

> In this exercise the performers attempt to convey as much meaning as possible without the use of dialogue.

Suitable for

KS3, KS4

Aims

- To develop story and plot.
- To convey emotions physically.
- To enhance spatial awareness.
- To create effective material working within a given structure.

Resources

- None

Space

- Suitable for use in the classroom

What to do

1. The majority of scenes in this section rely heavily on language. Most of the work created by young people contains a word count with no real consideration of what is actually being said. This exercise concentrates more on 'show' rather than 'tell'.

2. The scenes below should be acted out without the use of dialogue, in complete silence. The aim is to convey the essence of the scene and establish the Who, What, Where of the scene through body language and physical clues only.

3. Each scene should last no more than 2 minutes.

Care

A boy has finally contacted his real mum and they are meeting now at his foster parents' home.

The foster mother reluctantly plays host to the reunion.

The boy's real mother – who gave him up as a baby.

The boy's step-sister – they are very close and he has asked her to be there. She is worried that the boy will chose to leave to be with his real mother.

Hospital

The husband who fears the worst.

The daughter who believes her mother will be fine.

The mother has been positively diagnosed with a congenital illness – her daughter is likely to inherit.

War

A mother who lost her father in the war.

A son who is leaving home today to join the army.

His brother, same age, same wish but failed his medical.

Variation

Instead of letting a group rehearse their scene, give a group the premise as outlined above and have them perform it without preparation. See if the audience can work out what is happening and who the characters are in each of the scenes.

All of Me

All of Me is an exercise that allows you to visualise your potential. This exercise encourages you to write down every aspect of your character and consider when and how often you use particular parts of your 'self'.

Suitable for

KS3, KS4

Aims

- To develop information about character history.
- To enhance self-awareness.
- To understand individual and character personalities.

Resources

- None

Space

- Suitable for use in the classroom

What to do

1. This is a great way to get to know yourself.
2. Take a sheet of A4 paper and draw a circle in the centre. Write in that circle your name or simply the word 'Me'. This is the centre of a flower; you will now add the petals.
3. Draw a petal leading from the centre of your flower. Write inside that petal a word that describes a character trait of yours, it may be disorganised, it may be excitable, or simply fun. When you have filled in your first petal with a word repeat the process until the whole page is full.

4. If you can't fill the whole page, fill in as many petals as possible.

5. When you have finished sit and look at the final image. Re-read all the words in the flower and see the range of potential that is within you.

6. It's the facilitator's job to put this information to good use.

7. You could ask for the words to be separated into positive and negative traits and use this as a starting point for further discussion (you could even use the Agree/Disagree continuum as a way of opening up the discussion).

8. You could ask individuals to choose one trait/emotion and remember a time or event that generated that feeling within them. This event could then be re-enacted.

9. This is a powerful exercise and can lead to many possible developments.

10. Always remember, however, that it is sometimes difficult for people to express feelings or talk directly about themselves and as such, any developments are always safer when expressed dramatically.

Variation

- This exercise could also be used as a way of recording different sides of a character, providing an excellent structure for some detailed character analysis.

Writer's Raffle

> This is a writing exercise that forces the incorporation of existing lines into developing scenes.

Suitable for

KS3, KS4

Aims

- To develop spontaneity.
- To improve speaking and listening.
- To encourage more imaginative responses.
- To create effective material working within a given structure.
- To justify character actions.

Resources

- 'Location' cards
- Lines of dialogue written on slips of paper
- A hat or container (see the back of this book for locations and suitable lines of dialogue)

Space

- Suitable for use in the classroom

What to do

1. This exercise can be done individually or you could split the group into 2s, 3s or 4s.

2. The facilitator should have prepared a series of cards with location names written on them (choose from the 'locations' listed at the back of this book, see p. 211). Ask each person (or team) to choose a location. Their job is to write a scene set in the location they have chosen.

3. The facilitator has also prepared a number of slips of paper with lines of dialogue written on them (these can also be found at the back of this book, see p. 207). The slips of paper should be folded and placed into a hat or container from where they can be selected (rather like a raffle).

4. Each writer (or team of writers) should select six lines of dialogue. These lines must then be incorporated in their script, set in the location they have already selected.

5. Finished scenes should last no longer than three minutes.

Variation

- If this exercise is being carried out by groups of writers, print out the finished scripts and hand them to another group whose challenge is to perform the scene for the rest of the class.

What's so Funny?

What's so Funny? calls for serious acting. Can the players hold it together and create a dramatic scene or will the audience break into fits of laughter?

Suitable for

KS3, KS4

Aims

- To enhance concentration.
- To improve speaking and listening.
- To create story and plot.

Resources

- None

Space

- Suitable for use in the classroom

What to do

1. This exercise is best played in small groups.
2. Ask 6–8 players to volunteer. Two of the volunteers begin on stage as performers, the others wait at the side of the stage for their turn.
3. The two performers start an improvised scene (use locations, relationships or starting lines for inspiration). The aim of the exercise is to make the scene as serious as possible.
4. Whenever somebody in the audience laughs, the performer they laughed at leaves the stage and is replaced by somebody waiting on the sidelines.
5. This is a great exercise to explore what makes something funny and for performers to experiment with gravitas and sincerity.

Emotional Baggage

Emotional Baggage is an exercise that helps performers display an emotion precisely to both the audience and their fellow actors.

Suitable for

KS3, KS4

Aims

- To develop spontaneity.
- To improve speaking and listening.
- To convey emotions physically.
- To justify character actions.

Resources

- None

Space

- Suitable for use in the classroom

What to do

1. This exercise is best played by 4 people.
2. Three performers play passengers and the other plays an airport security guard.
3. The facilitator takes the passengers to one side and gives them an emotion to work with (e.g. anger, lust, fear).
4. Each passenger has to walk through the airport check point to have their bags checked. They strike up a conversation with the security guard for as long as it takes for the guard to guess the emotion they have been given.
5. Once the emotion has been guessed the passenger passes through the check point and the next person approaches.

Appendices

First and Last Lines

The lines contained in this section are provided as a starting, or end point, for the scenes you are working on. Use them to kick start the imagination and to provide structure to the work you are developing. They will be particularly useful when beginning to write and will hopefully provide an inspiring starting point for scripts, scenes and monologues.

Ah, that's better.
Alice asked me to give you a message.
All those eyes looking at me, it was hideous.
Are these yours?
Are you sure this fits me?
Bring me my trumpet.
Can I come in?
Can I trust you?
Do you need some help with that?
Do you think this is easy for me?
Don't look at me like that!
Don't touch me!
Every time I think about you it makes me smile.
Great, now everyone will know!
Great, now we're both going to get in trouble!
I brought you here for a reason.
I can tell you hate me!
I can't believe you just did that!
I can't remember that.
I guess it's my lucky day!
I hope you're going to pay for that!
I think we're here.
I turned around and guess what I saw?
I'm afraid the game's up.
I'm in trouble.
I'm leaving you.
I'm pregnant.
I'm your father.
I've got the results.
I've never felt like this before.
I've never felt so alone.
I've never noticed that before.
If you've got something to say, say it!
Is it still there?
Is there anything else you can do?
Is this yours?
It seems like everything I do is wrong!
It's a disaster!
It's all going wrong!

It's booked. I hope you're ready?

It's broken.

It's so beautiful.

It's unbelievable!

Keep away from me!

Keep your mouth shut!

Let me read that.

Let's get out of here while we can.

Like mother, like daughter.

Mum and Dad would have been so proud.

Of course I'm confused who wouldn't be?

Put that down, it's got nothing to do with you!

Rules are meant to be broken.

Say it again.

Sssh! Did you hear that?

Stand back!

Stop, take a deep breath and count to ten.

Take it, it's all yours.

Take my hand.

Thanks for looking after me.

That's a fantastic idea!

This feels great!

This has to be the worst day of my life.

This is the final straw!

Tomorrow is just another day.

Tomorrow let's do something nice.

Trust me I'm never going back there.

We might as well give up.

Well make your mind up, it's either one or the other.

What are you doing here?

What are you writing?

What goes around comes around.

What's this?

Where did you get that from?

Where have you been I've been waiting for you all night?

Which one should I cut first?

Who do you think you are?

Who'd have thought we'd get this far?

Will you come with me tomorrow? I don't want to go on my own.

With time you'll come to forget.
You left this.
You might want to sit down.
You're back!
You're certainly a chip off the old block.
You're fired!
You're the best thing that's ever happened to me.

Locations

When writing or starting scenes from scratch it can often help to have a location in mind, somewhere to set the action and give it an all important context. In this section I've provided a comprehensive, but not exhaustive, list of locations that can be used to fire your scenes into life. Use them on their own or couple them with a starting line from the previous section to give a definite structure to the work you are creating.

Abandoned warehouse
Aeroplane cockpit
Air-raid shelter
Airport
Alleyway
Allotment
Army barracks
Bank
Beach
Boat
Bridge
Bunker
Bus stop/Train station
Castle
Cave
Changing room
Church
Classroom
Courtroom
Desert/Desert island
Doctor's waiting room
Fishing lake
Forest/Woodland
Graveyard/Cemetery
Haunted house
Head Teacher's office
Hospital
Hostel
Hot-air balloon
Library
Lift/Elevator
Mine shaft
Mountain
Park bench
Playground
Prison/Police cell
Pub/Nightclub
Restaurant/Kitchen
Scene of an accident

Spaceship
Submarine
Supermarket
Theatre
Tomb
Train
Vets
Walk-in fridge
Waxwork museum
Zoo

Classroom Gems

Innovative resources, inspiring creativity across the school curriculum

Designed with busy teachers in mind, the Classroom Gems series draws together an extensive selection of practical, tried-and-tested, off-the-shelf ideas, games and activities, guaranteed to transform any lesson or classroom in an instant.

© 2008 Paperback 336pp
ISBN: 9781405873925

© 2008 Paperback 312pp
ISBN: 9781405859455

© 2009 Paperback 216pp
ISBN: 9781408220382

© 2009 Paperback 192pp
ISBN: 9781408225608

© 2009 Paperback 392pp
ISBN: 9781408223208

© 2009 Paperback 320pp
ISBN: 9781408228098

© 2009 Paperback 312pp
ISBN: 9781408223260

© 2009 Paperback 352pp
ISBN: 9781408223291

© 2009 Paperback 384pp
ISBN: 9781408224359

'Easily navigable, allowing teachers to choose the right activity quickly and easily, these invaluable resources are guaranteed to save time and are a must-have tool to plan, prepare and deliver first-rate lessons'

PEARSON